MACMILLAN MASTER GUIDES

GENERAL EDITOR: JAMES GIBSON

Published

JANE AUSTEN	*Emma* Norman Page
	Sense and Sensibility Judy Simons
	Pride and Prejudice Raymond Wilson
	Mansfield Park Richard Wirdnam
SAMUEL BECKETT	*Waiting for Godot* Jennifer Birkett
WILLIAM BLAKE	*Songs of Innocence* and *Songs of Experience* Alan Tomlinson
ROBERT BOLT	*A Man for all Seasons* Leonard Smith
EMILY BRONTË	*Wuthering Heights* Hilda D. Spear
GEOFFREY CHAUCER	*The Miller's Tale* Michael Alexander
	The Pardoner's Tale Geoffrey Lester
	The Prologue to the Canterbury Tales Nigel Thomas and Richard Swan
CHARLES DICKENS	*Bleak House* Dennis Butts
	Great Expectations Dennis Butts
	Hard Times Norman Page
GEORGE ELIOT	*Middlemarch* Graham Handley
	Silas Marner Graham Handley
	The Mill on the Floss Helen Wheeler
HENRY FIELDING	*Joseph Andrews* Trevor Johnson
E. M. FORSTER	*Howards End* Ian Milligan
	A Passage to India Hilda D. Spear
WILLIAM GOLDING	*The Spire* Rosemary Sumner
	Lord of the Flies Raymond Wilson
OLIVER GOLDSMITH	*She Stoops to Conquer* Paul Ranger
THOMAS HARDY	*The Mayor of Casterbridge* Ray Evans
	Tess of the d'Urbervilles James Gibson
	Far from the Madding Crowd Colin Temblett-Wood
JOHN KEATS	*Selected Poems* John Garrett
PHILIP LARKIN	*The Whitsun Weddings* and *The Less Deceived* Andrew Swarbrick
D. H. LAWRENCE	*Sons and Lovers* R. P. Draper
HARPER LEE	*To Kill a Mockingbird* Jean Armstrong
CHRISTOPHER MARLOWE	*Doctor Faustus* David A. Male
THE METAPHYSICAL POETS	Joan van Emden

MACMILLAN MASTER GUIDES

THOMAS MIDDLETON and WILLIAM ROWLEY	*The Changeling* Tony Bromham
ARTHUR MILLER	*The Crucible* Leonard Smith
GEORGE ORWELL	*Animal Farm* Jean Armstrong
WILLIAM SHAKESPEARE	*Richard II* Charles Barber *Hamlet* Jean Brooks *King Lear* Francis Casey *Henry V* Peter Davison *The Winter's Tale* Diana Devlin *Julius Caesar* David Elloway *Macbeth* David Elloway *Measure for Measure* Mark Lilly *Henry IV Part I* Helen Morris *Romeo and Juliet* Helen Morris *The Tempest* Kenneth Pickering *A Midsummer Night's Dream* Kenneth Pickering
GEORGE BERNARD SHAW	*St Joan* Leonée Ormond
RICHARD SHERIDAN	*The School for Scandal* Paul Ranger *The Rivals* Jeremy Rowe
ALFRED TENNYSON	*In Memoriam* Richard Gill
JOHN WEBSTER	*The White Devil* and *The Duchess of Malfi* David A. Male

Forthcoming

CHARLOTTE BRONTË	*Jane Eyre* Robert Miles
JOHN BUNYAN	*The Pilgrim's Progress* Beatrice Batson
JOSEPH CONRAD	*The Secret Agent* Andrew Mayne
T. S. ELIOT	*Murder in the Cathedral* Paul Lapworth *Selected Poems* Andrew Swarbrick
GERARD MANLEY HOPKINS	*Selected Poems* R. Watt
BEN JONSON	*Volpone* Michael Stout
RUDYARD KIPLING	*Kim* Leonée Ormond
ARTHUR MILLER	*Death of a Salesman* Peter Spalding
JOHN MILTON	*Comus* Tom Healy
WILLIAM SHAKESPEARE	*Othello* Tony Bromham *As You Like It* Kiernan Ryan *Coriolanus* Gordon Williams *Antony and Cleopatra* Martin Wine
ANTHONY TROLLOPE	*Barchester Towers* Ken Newton
VIRGINIA WOOLF	*To the Lighthouse* John Mepham *Mrs Dalloway* Julian Pattison
W. B. YEATS	*Selected Poems* Stan Smith

MACMILLAN MASTER GUIDES

SONGS OF INNOCENCE AND OF EXPERIENCE

BY WILLIAM BLAKE

ALAN TOMLINSON

MACMILLAN
EDUCATION

First edition 1987

Published by
MACMILLAN EDUCATION LTD
Houndmills, Basingstoke, Hampshire RG21 2XS
and London
Companies and representatives
throughout the world

Typeset by TecSet

Printed in Hong Kong

British Library Cataloguing in Publication Data
Tomlinson, Alan
Songs of innocence and songs of experience
by William Blake.—(Macmillan master
guides)
1. Blake, William, *1757–1827*. Songs of
innocence   2. Blake, William, *1757–1827*
Songs of experience
I. Title
821'.7   PR4144.S63
ISBN 0–333–41377–6 Pbk
ISBN 0–333–41378–4 Pbk export

CONTENTS

GENERAL EDITOR'S PREFACE

The aim of the Macmillan Master Guides is to help you to appreciate the book you are studying by providing information about it and by suggesting ways of reading and thinking about it which will lead to a fuller understanding. The section on the writer's life and background has been designed to illustrate those aspects of the writer's life which have influenced the work, and to place it in its personal and literary context. The summaries and critical commentary are of special importance in that each brief summary of the action is followed by an examination of the significant critical points. The space which might have been given to repetitive explanatory notes has been devoted to a detailed analysis of the kind of passage which might confront you in an examination. Literary criticism is concerned with both the broader aspects of the work being studied and with its detail. The ideas which meet us in reading a great work of literature, and their relevance to us today, are an essential part of our study, and our Guides look at the thought of their subject in some detail. But just as essential is the craft with which the writer has constructed his work of art, and this may be considered under several technical headings – characterisation, language, style and stagecraft, for example.

The authors of these Guides are all teachers and writers of wide experience, and they have chosen to write about books they admire and know well in the belief that they can communicate their admiration to you. But you yourself must read and know intimately the book you are studying. No one can do that for you. You should see this book as a lamp-post. Use it to shed light, not to lean against. If you know your text and know what it is saying about life, and how it says it, then you will enjoy it, and there is no better way of passing an examination in literature.

JAMES GIBSON

TEXTUAL NOTE

Any apparent oddities of spelling or word formation within the quotations in this Guide are Blake's own. He habitually wrote 'ie' after 'c' in such words as 'percieves' and 'recieved', and often used the symbol '&' instead of writing out 'and' in full. In typical eighteenth-century fashion he also liberally, if inconsistently, gave capital initial letters to some words when writing. Some editions remove these features and make Blake's text conform to modern usage, but there is little real practical necessity to do so and I have preferred to follow Blake's own usages. The standard complete edition, Geoffrey Keynes's *Compete Writings* (Oxford University Press, 1966), and one of the most widely used and highly recommendable selections, J. Bronowski's *Blake: Poems and Selected Writings* (Penguin, 1958), both use Blake's spelling.

ACKNOWLEDGEMENT

Cover illustration: *Pity* by William Blake. Photograph © Tate Gallery Publications Department.

1 WILLIAM BLAKE: LIFE AND BACKGROUND

William Blake was born in London on 28 November 1757, the second of five children of James Blake, a hosier, and his wife Catherine. This was not the 'poor background' maintained by some sentimental early admirers of Blake, but rather a solidly lower-middle-class one. The fact that Blake had little formal education, for instance, was probably due less to his family's inability to provide him with one than to his father's willingness to cater for his precocious artistic talents. In 1767, at the age of ten, Blake was enrolled in Henry Pars's drawing school in the Strand in the West End of London – one of the best and most fashionable preparatory schools for young artists. Here Blake was introduced to the study of ideal form by being set to draw from plaster casts of antique sculpture, and also to the pleasures and benefits of collecting prints of the work of great artists of the past.

Being an artist, however, was at best an uncertain profession, and in 1772 Blake was apprenticed to the engraver James Basire, from whom he learned a craft that would be more likely to provide him with steady employment. When this apprenticeship ended in 1779 Blake continued to study art for a while, at the newly-founded Royal Academy in London, but from that time to his death he largely supported himself and, after his marriage in 1782, his wife Catherine, by engraving and illustrating, work that was only occasionally supplemented by commissions for paintings. Except for a brief period from 1800 to 1803 when he and his wife lived in the Sussex village of Felpham, Blake spent his whole life in London, where he died on 12 August 1827, and he lived, worked, and died in relative obscurity.

Blake was as precocious a poet as he was an artist. When his first book, *Poetical Sketches*, was published in 1783, its preface claimed that 'The following sketches were the production of untutored youth, commenced in his twelfth, and occasionally resumed by the author till his twentieth year,' and that they had not been revised for this publication. If this is true the poems are often remarkably accomplished, and they justify the preface's belief 'that they possessed a poetic originality, which merited some respite from oblivion.' They are still immature works, though, in many ways conventional enough minor eighteenth-century poetry, and Blake's true 'poetic originality' really manifests itself six years later, with the publication of *Songs of Innocence* in 1789.

An important aspect of that 'originality' is that Blake is one of the first generation of Romantic poets. Romanticism in literature and the other arts was characterised by imagination and passion, appealing to the feelings rather than to the intellect. It was an artistically revolutionary movement, in that its followers set themselves against the essentially rational standards of taste that had governed the form and content of most eighteenth-century art, and it arose in association with actual political revolutions in the world at large, most importantly in America in 1776 and in France in 1789. Blake had walked the streets of London wearing the red cap that was the sign of the Jacobins, a political club established in Paris in 1789 to uphold and to promote the principles of absolute democracy and equality. By wearing the red cap Blake openly proclaimed himself an extreme radical, a sympathiser with the ideals of the French Revolution.

The appearance of *Songs of Innocence*, and the addition to them of *Songs of Experience* by 1794, make as good an occasion as any, and a better than most, to mark the beginnings of Romanticism in English literature. The publication by Wordsworth and Coleridge of their *Lyrical Ballads* in 1798 has sometimes been a preferred event, but by then Blake had written not only the *Songs* but also such things as *The Book of Thel* (1789), *The Marriage of Heaven and Hell* (somewhere between 1790 and 1793), *Visions of the Daughters of Albion* and *America, a Prophecy* (both 1793), and *The Book of Urizen* and *Europe, a Prophecy* (both 1794). For various reasons none of these had anything like the public impact of *Lyrical Ballads*, but they form a body of work in which some of the central elements of the Romantic ideology appear fully formed.

One aspect of how this ideology appears in Blake's work can cause problems for his readers, and may well have contributed to the incomprehension and neglect with which so much of his work was met. Blake was a religious artist but, like so many of the Romantics, he deeply distrusted the doctrines and practices of the conventional, orthodox Christianity of his time. In 'The Garden of Love' in *Songs of Experience* he writes of how

A Chapel was built in the midst,
Where I used to play on the green.

And the gates of this Chapel were shut,
And 'Thou shalt not' writ over the door;
So I turn'd to the Garden of Love
That so many sweet flowers bore;

And I saw it was filled with graves,
And tomb-stones where flowers should be;
And Priests in black gowns were walking their rounds,
And binding with briars my joys & desires.

This is not an anti-religious poem but an anti-clerical one: Blake sees organised, establishment religion as implicated in the morally and spiritually repressive practices of the establishment. Instead of helping people to discover themselves and their potential, it tries to deny them the opportunities for doing so.

Blake seems to have felt that he could only freely use the images and narrative patterns of Christianity in his work once he had liberated them from their association with establishment orthodoxy and made them his own. Accordingly, in his writings of this period he begins to invent a personal myth, recognisably based on the motifs and traditions of Christianity, but reinterpreting and rearranging them so as to alter their significance for his own ends. We need not concern ourselves too much with the specific names and incidents of this myth, as they are largely irrelevant to the *Songs*, but the ideas that are being dramatised in it certainly are relevant to them. As we shall see, some of the characters also do lurk in the shadows of at least the *Songs of Experience*.

Even those few remarks about the peculiar private world of Blake's metaphors for poetry show that his art is, typically of Romanticism as a whole, revolutionary in terms of its social and political concerns as well as its artistic ones. In that brief list of some of Blake's works I have given above, *America, a Prophecy* is a visionary celebration of the successful American revolution, and *Europe, a Prophecy* contains a parable about the reactionary attempts to suppress the French Revolution or to pervert its course. The poem ends with a vision of how, nevertheless, the revolutionary spirit will triumph in Europe, on both the material and the mental planes of existence:

But terrible Orc, when he beheld the morning in the east,
Shot from the heights of Enitharmon,
And in the vineyards of red France appear'd the light of
    his fury . . . .
Then Los arose: his head he rear'd in snaky thunders clad;
And with a cry that shook all nature to the utmost pole,
Call'd all his sons to the strife of blood.

Amongst the symbolic characters of Blake's myth, Orc represents revolution in the material world, and is the first son of Los, who symbolises poetry, the expression in this world of the creative imagination. For Blake, the true poet is necessarily a revolutionary to some extent, for he tells the truth, about both how things are and how they could be. One of the 'Proverbs of Hell' in *The Marriage of Heaven and Hell* insists that 'Truth can never be told so as to be understood, and not be believ'd.' Such belief will affect how people act, and so change in the world is an all but inevitable consequence of the poet's expressing his visions.

It may not be going too far to find some of the reasons for the difference in tone between *Songs of Innocence* and *Songs of Experience* in Blake's own reactions to the French Revolution of 1789, its course and its consequences. In 1791 Blake began, but then abandoned, a poem in praise of *The French Revolution*. Much of it echoes the sunlit, optimistic joy that runs through so many of the *Songs of Innocence*:

> Then the valleys of France shall cry to the soldier: 'Throw
>   down thy sword and musket,
> And run and embrace the meek peasant.' Her nobles shall hear
>   and shall weep, and put off
> The red robe of terror, the crown of oppression, the shoes of
>   contempt, and unbuckle
> The girdle of war from the desolate earth; then the Priest in
>   his thund'rous cloud
> Shall weep, bending to earth, embracing the valleys, and
>   putting his hand to the plow,
> Shall say: 'No more I curse thee; but now I will bless thee; No
>   more in deadly black
> Devour thy labour . . . .'

Compare the vision expressed there with this, from 'The Chimnney Sweeper' in *Songs of Innocence*:

> And by came an Angel who had a bright key,
> And he open'd the coffins & set them all free;
> Then down a green plain leaping, laughing, they run,
> And wash in a river, and shine in the Sun
>
> Then naked & white, all their bags left behind,
> They rise upon clouds and sport in the wind;
> And the Angel told Tom, if he'd be a good boy,
> He'd have God for his father, & never want joy.

The French Revolution was to have been published by the radical bookseller Joseph Johnson, and was announced as 'A Poem in Seven Books', but only the first book has survived, as a set of printer's page proofs, so it was never published and Blake does not seem to have written any of the projected remainder of it. He may have abandoned the poem, partly because he was already disillusioned with the course events were taking, and by the completion of *Songs of Experience* in 1794 the Revolution had slipped into what became known as the 'Reign of Terror', during which the revolutionary government sought to impose its will through a series of show trials and mass executions, and France was embarked upon a European war that was beginning to look more like one of conquest than one of self-defence. Blake did not repent of his revolutionary enthusiasms, or recant them, but his vision had darkened and had turned more towards how things still were than how they might become.

But the main thrust of high Romantic thinking is towards ways of transforming or transcending the human condition, not towards the realistic appraisal of it (unless, of course, that helps in seeing how to transform it). We find in Blake's writings a characteristic Romantic emphasis on the importance of personal growth, inspired and directed by the imaginative ability to learn, creatively, from individual experience. The basic assumption is that people learn best from their own experiences, not from precept or instruction or reason:

The road of excess leads to the palace of wisdom.
No bird soars too high, if he soars with his own wings.
The eagle never lost so much time as when he submitted to learn of the crow.
You never know what is enough unless you know what is more than enough.

At least the first and third of those selected 'Proverbs of Hell' also imply the related Romantic belief in the perfectibility of human beings. If men and women are given the radical personal freedom necessary for the experiment, the freedom to 'persist' in their 'folly' if need be, then they can raise themselves higher than mere reason, and the regimentation of their activities that it gives rise to, would ever allow.

Near the beginning of *The Marriage of Heaven and Hell* Blake lists these three 'Errors' which have been caused by 'All Bibles or sacred codes':

1. That Man has two real existing principles: Viz: Body & a Soul.
2. That Energy, call'd Evil, is alone from the Body; & that Reason, call'd Good is alone from the Soul.
3. That God will torment Man in Eternity for following his Energies.

Blake's main purpose here is to attack what he takes to be the conventional notion of 'Reason' as some kind of channel for divinely-ordained, absolute standards and values, a prescriber of limits for human beings. He opposes to his three errors 'the following contraries':

1. Man has no Body distinct from his Soul, for that call'd Body is a portion of Soul discern'd by the five Senses, the chief inlets of Soul in this age.
2. Energy is the only life, and is from the Body; and reason is the bound or outward circumference of Energy.
3. Energy is Eternal Delight.

In the second of these propositions Blake is asserting that reason does not set limits to the activity of human energy, but is itself ever being pushed out to new limits by that energy. At any one time what it is 'reasonable' to believe human beings are capable of is the very utmost that they have yet aspired to. One of the 'Proverbs of Hell' points out that 'What is now proved was once only imagin'd.' A few lines later Blake builds on this to claim that 'Every thing possible to be believ'd is an image of truth.' Whatever the human imagination can conceive of the human will can create – or at least something very like it. That proverb is then followed by one quoted earlier:

The eagle never lost so much time as when he submitted to learn of the crow.

The inference is clear: no one else can really say whether something is or is not possible for you; you must attempt it for yourself, and discover.

The Romantics formed such beliefs as a critical reaction to the empirical rationalism of the Enlightenment, that 'Age of Reason' that gave eighteenth-century culture its characteristic tone. The thinkers of the Enlightenment also held that knowledge derived from experience, but in a purely mechanical fashion. Their theories left no room for the workings of that creative imagination that Blake called 'The Divine Vision' (in a marginal note written in 1826 in a copy of the 1815 edition of Wordsworth's *Poems*), and which, in his view, fed the mind with visions of new experiences,inspiring the will to realise them in actual experiences. The Scottish philosopher and historian David Hume wrote in his *Enquiry Concerning Human Understanding* (1748):

> But though our thought seems to possess this unbounded liberty, we shall find . . . that it is really confined within very narrow limits, and that all this creative power of the mind amounts to no more than the faculty of compounding, transposing, augmenting, or diminishing the materials afforded us by the senses and experience.

It is important to distinguish this from Blake's view of how people learn from experience. He holds that the creative imagination, possessed of exactly 'this unbounded liberty' that Hume denies, conceives of something new, something that has not yet existed or been done, and the experience from which people then learn is the experience of trying to do it, to make it become true.

Blake summarised what he saw as the logical consequence of the typical Enlightenment view, as stated by Hume, in the sets of aphorisms that he published in 1788 as *There is No Natural Religion* and *All Religions are One*. In *All Religions are One* he writes:

> As none by travelling over known lands can find out the unknown,
> So from already acquired knowledge Man could not acquire more:
> therefore an universal Poetic Genius exists.

If there were no 'Poetic Genius,' no creative imagination with its ability to invent the new, there could be no access to new knowledge, no new ideas. The reasoning is spelled out in the First Series of *There is No Natural Religion*:

> V. Man's desires are limited by his perceptions, none can desire what he has not perciev'd.
> VI. The desires & perceptions of man, untaught by any thing but organs of sense, must be limited to objects of sense.
> *Conclusion.* If it were not for the Poetic or Prophetic character the Philosophic & Experimental would soon be at the ratio of all things, & stand still, unable to do other than repeat the same dull round over again.

That this has not happened is, as the first two aphorisms of the Second Series assert, because:

I.   Man's perceptions are not bounded by organs of perception; he perceives more than sense (tho' ever so acute) can discover.
II. Reason, or the ratio of all we have already known, is not the same that it shall be when we know more.

2 BLAKE'S PRINTING METHODS

Only one of Blake's literary works was published by conventional means – set in metal type and printed – during his lifetime, his first book, *Poetical Sketches* (1783). *The French Revolution* was to have been so published in 1791, but does not seem ever to have been issued. All of his other published works were brought out by Blake himself in a unique form: as illustrated, hand-coloured texts, which he called 'Illuminated Books'.

Blake's term 'illuminated' is preferable to 'illustrated', which is a little misleading. His aim was not simply to provide a picture which would 'visualise' something in the text but be essentially separable from it. Rather, he sought to create a unity of visual and verbal design, words and images read and seen together as component parts of an integral whole. It is not just a matter of pictures being placed on the page with the text, or on a page facing it. A great variety of devices is used to decorate the text or to expand its significance: not just pictures, but also plants and foliage, groups of animal and human figures, which twine themselves in and out of the words, joining some together, separating others. He also used washes of different colours behind the words, suggesting feelings which then attach themselves to those passages.

Blake did not do this lightly, for the technique of producing the 'Illuminated Books' was complicated and exacting. Blake outlined his design for a page onto a copper plate, drawing with a varnish that would resist the corrosive action of acid. When the plate was then put into a bath of acid, the unprotected metal was eaten away, leaving the design, once both acid and varnish had been washed off, standing out in high relief. This high relief part of the plate could then be inked, so as to print the design onto a sheet of paper pressed against the plate. The design on the plate would, of course, be a mirror image of what it printed on the paper, which means that the text, if applied directly to the plate, would have had to be written backwards – a very difficult procedure! Instead, Blake probably wrote the text, using acid-resistant varnish, on a sheet of paper which he had first coated with a sticky gum. The copper plate was then heated and the paper pressed against it for a while so that it would leave a reversed image on the surface of the plate. Blake printed off pages from such plates and then coloured them by hand, mostly in water colours, using diluted carpenter's glue to 'bind' the colours, making them more permanent and more resistant to the wear and tear caused by readers handling the books.

An obvious consequence of this method of book production is that no two copies of any one page will ever be identical. The basic design remains the same, but the colouring will vary from one copy to another. In fact, Blake often made substantial and deliberate changes in his designs over the years, painting in details that were not part of the original design, or painting out ones that were. In the design that accompanies 'The Lamb' in *Songs of Innocence* the little boy is usually naked, but in some copies he is clothed. So, although the designs are relevant to the interpretation of the text, the nature of that interpretation may vary according to which copy is being considered. The published text itself is not necessarily fixed, as Blake could, and did, experiment with different arrangements of it. Twenty-one copies of *Songs of Innocence* by themselves and 27 copies of the combined *Songs of Innocence and of Experience* (Blake does not seem ever to have issued *Songs of Experience* by themselves) are known to exist. Between them these copies offer 34 different arrangements of *Songs of Innocence* and 18 of *Songs of Experience*, with several poems that were originally in the *Innocence* sequence being transferred to *Experience*. The order conventionally adopted in modern editions of the poems (and followed in this book) is really only a matter of convenience, being the order that Blake seems to have settled down to in his later years, and should not be thought of as being necessarily of greater significance than other orders which he tried.

Blake had various motives for adopting this unusual and demanding practice. Some of them were simply practical: given both the style of his work, and his uncompromising and awkward personality, he might well have found it difficult to achieve publication through normal commercial channels. *Poetical Sketches* had been published through the patronage of some of Blake's friends, the sculptor John Flaxman and a noted literary and artistic hostess of the time, the wife of the Reverend A. S. Matthews, who between them bore the cost of publication. But by the time Blake was ready to issue *Songs of*

Innocence Flaxman was abroad, Mrs Matthews was no longer so close, or so willing, and Blake did not have the funds to subsidise publication himself. In the 1793 *Prospectus* which lists the works, both etched and engraved, that Blake had for sale, he complains that 'The Labours of the Artist, the Poet, the Musician, have been proverbially attended by poverty and obscurity' because they lacked the means to 'publish their own works.' He continues:

This difficulty has been obviated by the Author of the following productions now presented to the Public; who has invented a method of printing both Letter-Press and Engraving in a style more ornamental, uniform, and grand, than any before discovered, while it produces works at less than one fourth of the expense.

Quite apart from its convenience, Blake seems to have believed that the method could be highly profitable. He claimed that the idea of the Illuminated Books, and the technique by which to make them, had been revealed to him by the spiritual form of his younger brother Robert, a great favourite of his who had died in 1787 at the early age of nineteen (the first texts that Blake printed by the method were *There is No Natural Religion* and *All Religions are One*, both dating from about 1788), but there may also have been a more mundane source. Amongst Blake's close friends for many years was a London insurance agent and amateur artist named George Cumberland. Blake had helped Cumberland to etch plates from his own designs, and Cumberland had had the idea of printing poems from etched plates by 1784, when he wrote to his brother:

It is the amusement of an evening and is capable of printing 2000 if I wanted them – you see here one page which is executed as easily as writing and the Cost is trifling for your Copper is worth at any rate near as much as it cost besides you are not obliged to print any more than you want at one time, so that if the Work don't take you have nothing to do but to cut the Copper to pieces or clean it. – But if it does, you may print 4 editions, 2000 and then sell the Plates as well.

Around 1784 Blake worked on a satirical novel which he never finished but which has survived in manuscript. It is known as *An Island in the Moon*. Near the end, after a tantalising break where a page has been lost, there comes this prophetic, but also reminiscent, passage:

> – thus Illuminating the Manuscript.'
> 'Ay,' said she, 'that would be excellent.'
> 'Then,' said he, 'I would have all the writing Engraved instead of Printed, & at every other leaf a high finish'd print – all in three Volumes folio – & sell them a hundred pounds apiece. They would print off two thousand.'

Blake would seem to have believed that at one stroke he could free himself from the tyranny and timidity of publishers and patrons, and make a handsome profit!

But these were very far from being Blake's only motives. As the 1793 *Prospectus* proudly states, Blake considered himself the inventor of 'a method of Printing which combines the Painter and the Poet' and 'exceeds in elegance all former methods'. Text and design support and depend upon each other, as Blake points out in a letter of 1818 to Dawson Turner, a banker and art collector from Yarmouth:

> I send you a list of the different Works you have done me the honour to enquire after . . . Those I printed for Mr Humphry are a selection from the different Books of such as could be Printed without the Writing, tho' to the Loss of some of the best things. For they when Printed perfect accompany Poetical Personifications & Acts, without which Poems they never could have been Executed.

How the designs 'accompany' the poems can be suggested by a short discussion of the two complementary poems, one in *Songs of Innocence*, the other in *Songs of Experience*, called 'Nurse's Song'. The *Innocence* Nurse is permissive, her reaction when the children resist her calls of 'come home, my children,' and 'Come, come, leave off play,' being:

> 'Well, well, go & play till the light fades away
> And then go home to bed.'
> The little ones leaped & shouted & laugh'd
> And all the hills ecchoed.

In the illustration she sits apart and reading to herself under an apple tree while the children dance in a ring, their hands joined except where a break in their circle near her enables the viewer to see her as being symbolically included in it, sharing in their happiness. In contrast, the *Experience* Nurse is a stern disciplinarian to whom play is a frivolous waste of time:

> Your spring & your day are wasted in play,
> And your winter and night in disguise.

In the illustration to this poem a geometrically rigid doorway frames – confines, effectively – the three figures that are shown: the Nurse; a primly-dressed boy who stands still, his hands folded in front of him, while she combs his hair; and a girl who sits behind them apparently reading to herself, but still confined within the frame of the doorway.

This regimentation is fought against by nature, in the shape of vines laden with bunches of grapes, that grow up the sides of the doorframe and send out tendrils across its edges. But those vines and their grapes could also have another, more negative, significance. Vines feature in the decoration of the *Innocence* poem, too, where a vine is shown twining itself around a young elm tree on the opposite side of the children's play space from the Nurse's apple tree. In his *The Illuminated Blake* David V. Erdman suggests that the fact that 'No apples or grapes are indicated' means that 'happiness is in the present play.' The children are being allowed to be themselves, to savour their innocent joy to the full without being worried to take thought for the future. Those heavy clusters of vines in the *Experience* design would then clearly have the opposite significance: these children *are* being made to conform, literally 'groomed' (the Nurse's comb) for a settled place in an ordered society. The ripe fruit, the future that they must prepare for instead of wasting their time in play, could be seen to hem them in as oppressively as the straight lines of the doorframe do.

3 THEMES AND ISSUES

3.1 QUALITY OF VISION

In the *Descriptive Catalogue of Pictures . . . for Sale by Private Contract* that he had printed in 1809, Blake wrote:

> A Spirit and a Vision are not, as the modern philosophy supposes, a cloudy vapour, or a nothing: they are organized and minutely articulated beyond all that the mortal and perishing nature can produce. He who does not imagine in stronger and better lineaments, and in stronger and better light than his perishing and mortal eye can see, does not imagine at all.

Blake's visions are not supernatural visitations but intensifications of normal experience, heightenings of normal perception. Specifically, for Blake 'vision' was a way of seeing significance or value in things, rather than seeing only what he would have called their 'ratio', meaning the facts about those things, organised by the reason into a systematic form. Such seeing is both limited and limiting.

In *The Marriage of Heaven and Hell* Blake asks:

> How do you know but ev'ry Bird that cuts the airy way
> Is an immense world of delight, clos'd by your senses five?

Only by using the imagination to go beyond what the senses alone can reveal about a flying bird can someone observing it fully appreciate its true nature, what it does and how it does it. Another Romantic poet, John Keats, wrote in one of his letters:

> . . . if a Sparrow come before my Window I take part in its existence and pick about the Gravel.

Both Blake and Keats are writing of the same quality, and are even using similar examples to illustrate it, the quality that we call 'empathy' and that the poet Shelley called 'love' in his essay *A Defence of Poetry* (1821), where he defined it thus:

a going out of our own nature, and an identification of ourselves with the beautiful which exists in thought, action, or person, not our own.

That Blake, Keats, and Shelley can all be called as witnesses to the power and desirability of this frame of mind, and that all three of them identify the imagination as the mental faculty responsible for it, shows how widely such views were held in the Romantic period.

Blake thought of vision as operating on four distinct levels of intensity. He wrote about these four levels in a poem included in a letter of 1802 to his friend Thomas Butts, a London clerk who bought many of his works over the years:

> Now I a fourfold vision see,
> And a fourfold vision is given to me;
> 'Tis fourfold in my supreme delight
> And threefold in soft Beulah's night
> And twofold Always. May God us keep
> From Single vision & Newton's sleep!

'Single vision' is restricted to the facts of sensory experience, 'clos'd by your senses five,' and is not properly 'vision' at all. It is called 'Newton's sleep' because Blake liked to use Sir Isaac Newton, the greatest scientist England had ever produced, as an embodiment of the rational mind at its most deadening. Twofold vision is seeing beyond those basic facts, finding human value and significance in the things that are being perceived. Thus, in the poem to Butts:

> . . . before my way
> A frowning Thistle implores my stay.
> What to others a trifle appears
> Fills me full of smiles or tears;
> For double the vision my Eyes do see,
> And a double vision is always with me.
> With my inward Eye 'tis an old Man grey;
> With my outward, a Thistle across my way.

Seen with the 'inward Eye' of double vision the thistle in Blake's path becomes an old man trying to sow doubt and discouragement in his mind about the course his life is taking.

The next stage, 'in soft Beulah's night,' is threefold vision. In John Bunyan's allegorical novel *The Pilgrim's Progress* (1678), Beulah is an earthly paradise where those who have made a successful pilgrimage through the trials and tribulations of this world may live in happiness until the time comes for them to cross the river of death and enter heaven. In Blake's personal mythology Beulah is also a happy land, placed between eternity on the one hand and this world of organic matter on the other. Blake makes it a place of dreams and visions, and of the poetic inspiration that comes from dreams. He launches into the first book of his long poem *Milton* (1804) by making this appeal:

Daughters of Beulah! Muses who inspire the Poet's Song,
　　　　　. . . Come into my hand
By your mild power descending down the Nerves of my right arm
From out the Portals of my Brain, where by your ministry
The Eternal Great Humanity Divine planted his Paradise,
And in it caus'd the Spectres of the Dead to take sweet forms
In likeness of himself.

The 'Daughters of Beulah' are the inspirers of true poetry, which is why Blake writes of their power as 'descending down the Nerves of my right arm' to guide his writing hand. By locating their 'Realms/Of terror & mild moony lustre' within 'the Portals of my Brain' Blake makes it clear that they and the place the live in are imaginary, that they are, in fact, metaphors for the power of the creative imagination. The vision that belongs to this place, threefold vision, is creative vision, a state in which ideas directly express themselves as feelings, or even manifest themselves as objects or creatures.

Beyond this state lies the 'supreme delight' of fourfold vision, when imagination penetrates to the inmost essence of what is being perceived, and perception is illuminated by knowledge of the true reality of its object. It is a state of visionary ecstasy in which the world of eternity becomes real and present.

This 'eternity' of Blake's is not to be thought of as some kind of infinite extension of ordinary time. Rather, it is when any one individual moment is perceived with such fullness and intensity that it seems to become a moment outside ordinary time, and to last for ever. Near the end of the first book of *Milton* Blake considers such moments of intensity, and how they transcend time:

Every Time less than a pulsation of the artery
Is equal in its period & value to Six Thousand Years,
For in this Period the Poet's Work is Done, and all the Great
Events of Time start forth & are conciev'd in such a Period,
Within a Moment, a Pulsation of the Artery.

Later, in the second book, there is a passage where he suggests the possible rewards of cultivating such moments:

There is a Moment in each Day that Satan cannot find,
Nor can his Watch Fiends find it; but the Industrious find
This Moment & it multiply, & when it once is found
It renovates every Moment of the Day if rightly placed.

Cultivating 'vision' by continually exercising the imagination will give access to a state of mind in which 'the whole creation will be consumed and appear infinite and holy, whereas it now appears finite & corrupt.' Those words are from *The Marriage of Heaven and Hell*, where a little later Blake asserts that 'If the doors of perception were cleansed every thing would appear to man as it is, infinite.'

Blake consciously dedicated his art to the 'great task' of helping his fellow men to achieve in their own lives this cleansing of 'the doors of perception.' In the first chapter of *Jerusalem* (his final epic poem and the last major work that he printed by his process of relief etching; he worked on it between 1804, the date on the title page, and 1820, when the etching and the first printing were actually completed) Blake tells of how his friends are astonished at his distracted state of mind:

Yet they forgive my wanderings. I rest not from my great task!
To open the Eternal Worlds, to open the immortal Eyes
Of Man inwards into the Worlds of Thought, into Eternity
Ever expanding in the Bosom of God, the Human Imagination.

Blake can even claim, in *The Marriage of Heaven and Hell*, a symbolic appropriateness for his unique printing method, the use of acid to etch a metal plate:

this I shall do by printing in the infernal method, by corrosives, which in Hell are salutary and medicinal, melting apparent surfaces away, and displaying the infinite which was hid.

3.2 CONTRARY STATES

Blake has several stratagems for achieving this melting away of the deceptive surface appearances of things, most of which involve stimulating or provoking his readers into looking at things differently from how they normally do. To this end he will even tease the reader with deliberate obscurity. In a letter of 1799 to a clergyman named John Trusler, who was considering employing him as an illustrator, Blake wrote:

> The wisest of the Ancients consider'd what is not too Explicit as the fittest for Instruction, because it rouzes the faculties to act.

It does people good to force them to think for themselves, to make them question their assumptions. This is why Blake writes in *The Marriage of Heaven and Hell* that 'Opposition is true friendship'. A couple of pages after that statement Blake claims that Emanuel Swedenborg (1688–1722 – a Swedish visionary whose ideas influenced Blake's, but from whom he also differed strongly over many things) 'has not written one new truth' but instead 'has written all the old falsehoods.' This was because

> He conversed with Angels who are all religious, & conversed not with Devils who all hate religion, for he was incapable thro' his conceited notions.

Smugly convinced of the rightness of his own beliefs Swedenborg would not consider any contrary views, and so he never learned anything new.

Indeed, Blake seems to believe that it is only possible to learn from others by reacting against what they say or do, for no two people ever see things in the same way as each other, and so the passive acceptance of another's view is a negative and meaningless act. In the letter to Trusler, Blake responds to Trusler's criticism of his designs by defending his right to see things in his own way:

> I see Every thing I paint In This World, but Every body does not see alike . . . The tree which moves some to tears of joy is in the Eyes of others only a Green thing that stands in the way. Some See Nature all Ridicule & Deformity, & by these I shall not regulate my proportions; & Some Scarce see Nature at all. But to the Eyes of the Man of Imagination, Nature is Imagination itself. As a man is, So he Sees.

One of the 'Proverbs of Hell' had already, and more bluntly, used the same example to make the same point:

A fool sees not the same tree that a wise man sees.

And about 1803, in an unpublished poem called 'The Mental Traveller', Blake would write that 'the Eye altering alters all.' It is not only opinion that is subjective: perception itself is unique and personal to each individual. So you cannot adopt another's viewpoint, you can only encounter it and react to it.

If that should seem a contradiction of the remarks in section 3.1 about the desirability, even the necessity, of cultivating imaginative empathy, the power to transcend the confines of your own selfhood and to identify yourself with another, then the contradiction is more apparent than real. After all, you cannot encounter someone else's viewpoint in any very significant way if you are not fully aware of what it is. In order to become thus aware you must be able to conceive of other people's holding views which differ from your own, but which are equally valid for them, equally sincerely held. Otherwise you will be as blindly 'conceited' in holding to your own 'notions' as Blake thought Swedenborg was. To quote one of the 'Proverbs of Hell':

The crow wish'd every thing was black, the owl that every thing was white.

So recognition of the existence and the importance of alternatives – he called them 'contraries' – is fundamental to Blake's thinking, to his conception of human growth and learning. He set a statement of this principle near the very beginning of *The Marriage of Heaven and Hell*:

Without Contraries is no progression. Attraction and Repulsion, Reason and Energy, Love and Hate, are necessary to Human existence.

The character of Blake's thinking is essentially dialectical, in that it depends upon the interaction of contradictory or opposite forces. More than that, he is essentially a relativist. As the statement quoted above shows, any quality needs the existence of its contrary in order that it itself may exist. Without a knowledge of hate we could not know what love is; good could not meaningfully exist except as something distinguished from, defined against, evil.

Later in the *Marriage* Blake develops this argument by way of a division of human nature between two impulses:

Thus one portion of being is the Prolific, the other the Devouring: to the Devourer it seems as if the producer was in his chains; but it is not so, he only takes portions of existence and fancies that the whole.

But the Prolific would cease to be Prolific unless the Devourer, as a sea, recieved the excess of his delights.

It might be thought self-evident that to create is better than to destroy, and certainly the destructive impulse would eventually annihilate itself if the creative process were not there to continue to feed it. But, Blake argues, it is equally true that the creative impulse would have no motive to continue without the destructive process, and, if it did so, it would soon bury itself with its own productions. Therefore, he concludes that

These two classes of men are always upon earth, & they should be enemies: whoever tries to reconcile them seeks to destroy existence.

Life itself depends upon the interaction of contraries, the conflict of opposites. The cosmic drama that is played out in the first chapter of *Jerusalem* revolves around the dangers of trying to 'reconcile' such contraries instead of allowing them to work themselves out:

And this is the manner of the Sons of Albion in their strength:
They take the Two Contraries which are call'd Qualities, with
    which
Every Substance is clothed: they name them Good & Evil;
From them they make an Abstract, which is a Negation
Not only of the Substance from which it is derived,
A murderer of its own Body, but also a murderer
Of every Divine Member: it is the Reasoning Power,
An Abstract objecting power that Negatives every thing.
This is the Spectre of Man, the Holy Reasoning Power,
And in its Holiness is closed the Abomination of Desolation.

In Blake's symbolism the Spectre is the rational power of man, divided from any emotional or imaginative qualities and so, significantly, unable to sympathise with any other person. 'The Spectre of Man' is, therefore, a totally self-centred selfhood. In the quoted passage this state arises from a failure to realise that all existence is necessarily organised as a system of interacting contraries, all of which are equally valid, and an attempt to substitute for that vital conflict a rational – and so, inevitably, dead – abstraction.

3.3 INNOCENCE AND EXPERIENCE

The contraries of primary concern to us here, of course, are the states of innocence and experience. The title page that Blake designed for combined editions of the *Songs of Innocence and of Experience* carries a subtitle, 'Shewing the Two Contrary States of the Human Soul', and many an *Experience* poem is designed as the deliberate antithesis of an *Innocence* one. Thus 'The Lamb' of *Innocence* is confronted by 'The Tyger' of *Experience*, or the reader is offered two sharply contrasted views of the 'Holy Thursday' ceremonies in London's St Paul's Cathedral. The 'Holy Thursday' example is an especially useful one because a comparison of the two poems makes it so clear that what we are being given is two different ways of seeing the same event, two observers, neither of whom sees in the same way as the other does. Innocence and experience are essentially different ways of seeing, different kinds, or qualities, of vision.

In 'Auguries of Innocence', an unpublished poem written around 1803, Blake effectively defines at least the first of these qualities. The word 'auguries' means signs or tokens, and the form of the poem suggests that it is the first four lines which state what those signs of innocence are. They are separated from the rest of the poem by the fact that they make up a quatrain with an ABAB rhyme scheme, which is then followed by 64 rhyming couplets. That quatrain defines innocence as the ability

> To see a World in a Grain of Sand
> And a Heaven in a Wild Flower,
> Hold Infinity in the palm of your hand
> And Eternity in an hour.

This is imaginative vision, the fourfold vision that makes eternity a living reality to the human mind. In the first chapter of *Jerusalem* Blake, as the inspired poet-prophet possessed by 'my awful Vision', writes:

> I see the Four-fold Man . . .
> I see the Past, Present & Future existing all at once
> Before me.

In the 'Introduction' to *Songs of Experience* the reader is called upon to

> Hear the voice of the Bard!
> Who Present, Past, & Future, sees;
> Whose ears have heard
> The Holy Word
> That walk'd among the ancient trees . . .

This is vision that sees everything at once and sees it whole, unlike the partial vision of the deceived 'Devourer' of *The Marriage of Heaven and Hell* who 'only takes portions of existence and fancies that the whole.'

That partial vision is what lies behind much of the imagery in that sequence of rhyming couplets that makes up the bulk of 'Auguries of Innocence'. The mind, the imagination, that cannot see things whole, see the connections between things rather than the superficial differences between them, is a mind that is closed to the 'immense world of delight' created by 'ev'ry Bird that cuts the airy way.' Such a mind, its perceptions limited to the facts of sensory data, is caught in the trap described by Blake eight lines from the end of 'Auguries of Innocence':

> We are led to Believe a Lie
> When we see not Thro' the Eye.

Around 1810, drafting a prose essay which sets out to explain the symbolism of his painting of the Last Judgment, Blake enlarges upon this idea:

> I assert for My Self that I do not behold the outward Creation & that to me it is hindrance & not Action; it is as the Dirt upon my feet, No part of Me. 'What,' it will be Question'd, 'When the Sun rises, do you not see a round disk of fire somewhat like a Guinea?' O no, no, I see an Innumerable company of the Heavenly host crying 'Holy, Holy, Holy is the Lord God Almighty.' I question not my Corporeal or Vegetative Eye any more than I would Question a Window concerning a Sight. I look thro' it & not with it.

The mind that fails thus to see 'through' the eye, to look beyond the bare facts and imaginatively to 'see' their significant consequences, can, in 'Auguries of Innocence', accept, say, cruelty to animals, without realising that such behaviour betrays not just lack of concern but radical spiritual impoverishment. The inability to respond sympathetically to other creatures, or to other people, is what enables man to abuse them, not realising that thereby he harms himself, poisoning his own life and the world in which he lives it:

> A dog starv'd at his Master's Gate
> Predicts the ruin of the State . . . .
> Each outcry of the hunted Hare
> A fibre from the Brain does tear . . . .
> The Babe that weeps the Rod beneath
> Writes Revenge in realms of death . . . .
> The Soldier, arm'd with Sword & Gun,
> Palsied strikes the Summer's Sun.

Whole vision, the 'Divine Vision' of imagination, that would be able to perceive that such things are true and be moved to act in accordance with that perception, is vision inspired by strong faith. That does not mean religious faith, but, rather, faith in oneself, a trusting in the truth and the value of one's own experiences and imaginings. Given such faith anything is possible, as Blake says in *The Marriage of Heaven and Hell*:

> Then I asked: 'does a firm perswasion that a thing is so, make it so?'
> He replied: 'All poets believe that it does, & in ages of imagination this firm perswasion removed mountains; but many are not capable of a firm perswasion of any thing.'

Blake, founding the dialectical tensions of innocence and experience on these ideas, could be said to have created the primary symbolic antithesis of the *Songs* by following the example of Christ, who had equated true faith with the faith of a child. In the tenth chapter of St Mark's Gospel, Jesus's disciples try to prevent some children from approaching him:

> But when Jesus saw it, he was much displeased, and said unto them, Suffer the little children to come unto me, and forbid them not: for of such is the kingdom of God. Verily I say unto you, Whosoever shall not receive the kingdom of God as a little child, he shall not enter therein.

So Blake finds his perfect image of potent imaginative faith in a child's readiness to believe in the primacy of his own subjective vision. Moreover, like Christ in the Gospel, Blake in 'Auguries of Innocence' rebukes those experienced elders who would teach the child to be reasonable:

> He who mocks the Infant's Faith
> Shall be mock'd in Age & Death,
> He who shall teach the Child to Doubt
> The rotting Grave shall ne'er get out.
> He who respects the Infant's faith
> Triumphs over Hell & Death.

In 1793 Blake engraved (not etched – the processes are quite different) and published a little book called *For Children: The Gates of Paradise*. It is an emblem book, a sequence of symbolic pictures, each with a short caption identifying its subject. About 25 years later he revised and enlarged the book and reissued it as *For the Sexes: The Gates of Paradise*. In both versions the eleventh emblem shows a naked youth with winged shoulders moving towards a rising sun. Behind him an old man, wearing spectacles but with his eyes apparently closed behind them, holds the youth's wings and tries to clip them with a large pair of scissors. In 1793 the caption simply read 'Aged Ignorance'. In the revised version Blake added to those two words: 'Perceptive Organs closed, their Objects close.' The symbolism seems clear enough. The child represents life unaffected by worldliness or by repression, bright with the promise of discovery. Such is the state of innocence. The state of experience is represented by 'Aged Ignorance', eyes closed to the light, and clipping the wings of youth. Innocence believes, and so sees. Experience doubts, and so is blind.

> He who Doubts from what he sees
> Will ne'er Believe, do what you Please.
> If the Sun & Moon should doubt,
> They'd immediately Go out.
>   ('Auguries of Innocence')

4 COMMENTARY ON

SONGS OF INNOCENCE AND

SONGS OF EXPERIENCE

4.1 INTRODUCTION

In discussing these poems the point of view from which any one of them is written, the context in which it appears, must never be ignored. Blake did not just collect together a number of poems, he designed two antithetical but complementary sequences of poems, so that, taken together, they show 'the two Contrary States of the Human Soul'. Whether an individual poem is a song of innocence or a song of experience will affect how it is interpreted.

This concern for context, however, is affected by two major considerations which have already been explained. The first is that there is no one definitive order for the poems in either sequence. The standard order, followed here, is but one amongst a number of possibilities. David V. Erdman even suggests in *The Illuminated Blake* that 'For each fresh reading of Blake one might try the *Songs* in a fresh arrangement.' So any statements about the significance of the placing of any one poem in relation to the others must take account of the fact that other arrangements would suggest other significances. The second consideration is that Blake seems to have intended that some *Songs of Experience* should be read as the specific antitheses of particular *Songs of Innocence*. I have treated these pairings of 'contrary' poems as such in my commentary rather than discussing the poems separately.

There is another point to be made before embarking upon the commentary, one that applies to the reading of all poetry but has, perhaps, a special relevance for Blake's *Songs*: never simply assume that the 'I' who speaks in any given poem, even the most seemingly subjective or personal of lyrics, is the poet. It is an assumption that can mislead, and it is safer to think of the 'I' as a persona, a fictitious character invented by the poet and made to say these things within a

situation that the poet has also invented. It is easy to see that this is
the case in some poems: in each 'Nurse's Song' it is a woman who
speaks although the poet is a man; in 'The Lamb' it is a child we hear
and not the adult poet. It is less clear in the case of a poem like
'London', where it is temptingly easy to identify the speaker, a
visionary seer with something of the Old Testament prophet about
both his language and his manner (designedly so – the poem contains
what looks like a deliberate allusion to the Book of the Prophet
Ezekiel), with Blake himself. But the 'I' of 'London' is as much a
fictitious persona as the 'I' of 'Nurse's Song' is. Part of the purpose of
that allusion to Ezekiel may be to enforce the recognition of that fact,
to distance William Blake from the speaker of the poem:

> I wander thro' each charter'd street,
> Near where the charter'd Thames does flow,
> And mark in every face I meet
> Marks of weakness, marks of woe.

In Blake's time the general reader would have been much more
familiar with the Bible than is likely to be the case now, and such a
reader would probably be reminded by those lines of the Book of
Ezekiel, chapter 9, verse 4.

> And the Lord said unto him, Go through the midst of the city,
> through the midst of Jerusalem, and set a mark upon the foreheads
> of the men that sigh and that cry for all the abominations that be
> done in the midst thereof.

So reminded, the reader would tend to think of the 'I' of the poem less
as any one specific individual, more as a certain, special, 'type' of
person.

In fact Blake has invented two basic, distinct – but
related – personae through whom his two sequences of poems are
communicated to the reader. The *Songs of Innocence* are introduced
and sung by the Piper, the *Songs of Experience* by the Bard. They are
two fictitious poets who are, effectively, the authors of 'their' poems.
All poets, whether 'Piping songs of pleasant glee' or speaking with
'the voice of the Bard', are inevitably, like Ezekiel, prophets, for 'the
Poetic or Prophetic character' are one and the same. The Piper and
the Bard can be thought of as two voices, two characters, of the one
poet. 'The Voice of the Ancient Bard' is, in the standard order, the
last of the *Songs of Experience*, but it was originally a song of
innocence and is found more often in that sequence, and placed early

in it. Both of these voices are, of course, Blake's, but the useful-
ness – and the importance – of this elaborate fiction is that it reminds
us that neither point of view is his. At least, not *finally* his. The
contraries of innocence and experience are not absolute but provi-
sional, a creative opposition out of whose tension new insights can be
generated.

4.2 SONGS OF INNOCENCE

Introduction
Introduction (*Songs of Experience*)
Earth's Answer (*Songs of Experience*)
The *Experience* 'Introduction' is not strictly a contrary of the
Innocence one, but it is complementary to it in that it fulfils the same
function. Both poems define the emotional conditions of the worlds
in which the poems that they introduce are set, so it makes sense to
consider them together. 'Earth's Answer' is also being discussed here
because it and 'Introduction' make up a single unit (and, whatever
variations there may be in the ordering of different copies of *Songs of
Experience*, 'Earth's Answer' always follows 'Introduction').
   The Piper introduces his songs explicitly as 'songs of pleasant glee'
which 'Every child may joy to hear.' He is himself a child of nature,
'Piping down the valleys wild,' playing on his pipe to make music
without words, which could be interpreted as emotional art, without
intellectual or rational content. It is at the prompting of the child he
meets that he first sings the song, so presumably setting words to it,
then finally writes it down, preserving it as a memory for future times
in which this innocence no longer exists. It is in the fourth stanza that
the child asks the Piper to sit down and write his songs 'In a book that
all may read', and perhaps it is significant that it is at that moment
that, the Piper tells us, 'he vanish'd from my sight'. If, as seems
likely, the child is an embodiment of innocence, his disappearance
from the poem at the point where the songs of innocence are about to
be recorded for posterity may well be hinting that the moment at
which you begin to look back on innocence and happiness, to try to
preserve them as memories, is the moment at which you realise you
have lost them. Thus the poem prophetically foreshadows the loss of
innocence in the gaining of experience. For all that, though, the song
specifically mentioned in it is 'a song about a Lamb' and the purpose
of recording these songs is that they may move other children to tears
of joy.

The Piper essentially lives in the present, and has to be prompted by the response of an audience to think of preserving his songs. The Bard 'Present, Past, & Future, sees'. He sings from a knowledge of the whole history of the human race, and of any one human life. He introduces the *Songs of Experience* by rehearsing the Biblical story of mankind's fall from a state of grace into one of sin in his own terms, as a fall from innocence (the secure light of faith and trust) into experience (the darkness of confusion and error). God, 'The Holy Word' that has the power to 'fallen, fallen light renew', seems unwilling to use that power of renewal unless 'the lapsed Soul' first turns back to him. As 'Earth's Answer' then shows, the imposing of that condition is unjust and divisive, a self-centred attempt to force another to give something – love – which is only meaningfully given if freely given:

> Selfish father of men!
> Cruel, jealous, selfish fear! . . .
> Selfish! vain!
> Eternal bane!
> That free Love with bondage bound.

Jealousy is motivated by a fear of losing the beloved and a selfish desire to possess the beloved. In Blake's works jealousy is a common attribute of the vengeful and tyrannically demanding Old Testament God whom he called Nobodaddy – nobody's father. In 'To Nobodaddy', an unpublished poem from a manuscript notebook in which Blake made the first drafts of many of the *Songs of Experience*, he is addressed as 'Father of Jealousy', and described as hiding himself in 'darkness & obscurity' in an attempt to intimidate and control his children. He is no true father because by such behaviour he forfeits respect and affection, although he tries to insist on them as his right as 'the Father of the ancient men.' In Blake's myth this god is named Urizen, and distinguished as a separate being from the true, loving, God the Father, whom he tries to supplant.

Urizen is the power of reason – 'The Holy *Word*' – trying to limit and control the 'eternal delight' of bodily energy, represented here by the sexual power of generation implicitly embodied in the female Earth. He has tried to control this power by restricting it to the hours of darkness:

> The starry floor,
> The wat'ry shore,
> Is giv'n thee till the break of day.

But the secrecy and shame that result from this restriction corrupt the act of love:

> Can delight,
> Chain'd in night,
> The virgins of youth and morning bear?

The syntax of that is a little obscure but it can be followed: 'Can the virgins of youth and morning bear delight [to be] chain'd in night?' Another unpublished poem in the same manuscript notebook referred to above makes the point more explicitly:

> Are not the joys of morning sweeter
> Than the joys of night?
> And are the vig'rous joys of youth
> Ashamed of the light?
>
> Let age & sickness silent rob
> The vineyards in the night;
> But those who burn with vig'rous youth
> Pluck fruits before the light.

That 'before' means 'in front of'. The fourth stanza of 'Earth's Answer' protests that all human life is unnaturally perverted by these restrictions, and the poem then ends with Earth's plea for the breaking of 'this heavy chain', not as a reward for conforming to another's conception of good behaviour, but as an act of generosity and love. However, this fallen world seems sadly lacking in those qualities.

The Shepherd
The poem makes an image of security and contentment out of a flock of sheep under the protection of their 'watchful' shepherd. The shepherd is happy in his work – 'How sweet is the Shepherd's sweet lot!' – and the relationship of parent to child is not, as is so often the case in *Experience*, one of stern repression but one of loving concern, for 'the lamb's innocent call' is answered by 'the ewe's tender reply'.

The Ecchoing Green
This poem resembles 'Nurse's Song' (and in two copies of *Songs of Innocence* that poem immediately precedes 'The Ecchoing Green' while in another copy it immediately follows it) in that it, too,

presents a situation where 'old folk' and playing children are in harmony with each other. The various adults (the illustrations show younger men and women as well as 'Old John, with white hair') remember the 'joys' of their own 'youth time' with an apparent sense of happy identification and, like the Nurse, allow the children to play until 'The sun does descend' and they are really 'ready for rest'. The last two lines of the poem might plausibly be argued to foreshadow a time when these children will also have grown out of mere 'sports' but not, in this context, with any suggestion of their being in any way forced to do so. The final illustration shows a completely harmonious group of young and old making its way home.

The Lamb
The Tyger (*Songs of Experience*)
Probably the most famous pair of contrary poems in the *Songs*. The lamb is a traditional symbol of innocence, often used as such in the Bible, especially in the New Testament where Christ is the Lamb of God, offered as a sacrifice to atone for the sins of mankind. Thus the Lamb symbolises God's love. The child who speaks in Blake's poem explicitly identifies Christ, the actual lamb to whom he speaks, and himself together as equal participants in an existence unified by gentleness and love:

> He is called by thy name,
> For he calls himself a Lamb.
> He is meek, & he is mild;
> He became a little child.
> I a child, & thou a lamb,
> We are called by his name.

In contrast, the tiger symbolises God's anger. The simplest point being made by the contrast is that the speaker of 'The Tyger' feels forced to question whether two so violently opposed qualities can exist together in one being:

> Did he who made the Lamb make thee?

On these terms the speaker's question betrays his naîve ignorance of the complexities of reality and the answer to it is 'yes'. Unable to make sense of what he sees, to face up to an aspect of reality, he is baffled and even frightened by it, as is shown by the fact that 'The Tyger' is made up of a series of unanswered questions, whereas the child in 'The Lamb' can confidently answer all of the questions that he asks.

The last four lines of 'Auguries of Innocence' are:

> God appears & God is Light
> To those poor Souls who dwell in Night,
> But does a Human Form Display
> To those who Dwell in Realms of day.

The truly enlightened, those who live in the light of knowledge, know that divinity is not something above and beyond human beings, ruling over them, but a potential level of achievement within them. Another song of innocence, 'The Divine Image', identifies as the qualities of divinity 'Mercy, Pity, Peace, and Love', points out that these are human qualities, and concludes that

> every man, of every clime,
> That prays in his distress,
> Prays to the human form divine . . .

Those who live in the darkness of ignorance ('the forests of the night), who cannot satisfactorily integrate the various aspects of their experience (as the child of 'The Lamb' can), come to see that experience as something which they cannot control for themselves, controlled by a power which they cannot understand but which they must submit to. So, it is a power which they find themselves fearing. The last stanza of 'The Tyger' is almost identical to the first. Just one word has been changed, in the last line where 'Could frame thy fearful symmetry' has become 'Dare frame thy fearful symmetry'. In his first drafts of the poem Blake had 'Dare' in the first stanza, too, but changed it to 'Could'. That change reinforces the suggestion of a development: from wondering how such a thing could be, the speaker moves to wondering what dreadful power would have dared to make it be. He is numbered amongst those who, in *The Marriage of Heaven and Hell*, have 'forgot that All deities reside in the human breast.'

But if we follow up the parallels between 'The Tyger', and the developed symbolism of Blake's mythology, we find that the tiger was not created by any god of love, but by Urizen. In *Europe, a Prophecy* the coming to power of reason spreads darkness and creates forests of error:

> Thought chang'd the infinite to a serpent, that which pitieth
> To a devouring flame; and man fled from its face and hid
> In forests of night . . . .

God, 'the infinite' and 'that which pitieth', comes to be seen as 'a tyrant crown'd', to be feared and hidden from. In *Vala, or The Four Zoas* (a long narrative poem that Blake worked on between 1795 and about 1804 without ever getting it into publishable form) Urizen's 'tygers roam in the redounding smoke/In forests of affliction'. Urizen had been the 'Prince of Light,/First born of Generation' ('Generation' here is the act of true love and the source of all active life), but when he was bidden to 'Go forth & guide' men he became angry and resentful because he would rather have ruled over them:

> 'I went not forth: I hid myself in black clouds of my wrath;
> I call'd the stars around my feet in the night of councils dark;
> The stars threw down their spears & fled naked away.
> We fell.'

The same imagery marks the creation of 'The Tyger' in the fifth stanza of that poem. Stars symbolise reason in Blake and are associated with Urizen.

All of which might suggest that the answer to 'Did he who made the Lamb make thee?' should actually be 'no'. But Urizen embodies one faculty of the human mind, given undue prominence, and allowed to usurp or suppress the proper functions of other faculties. In the narrative of the myth his creations are his alone, but in terms of what the myth symbolises they are amongst the many creations of the complex human mind. So the answer can still be 'yes'. Especially as both 'The Lamb' and 'The Tyger' do not present objective descriptions of those creatures: they present human responses to them. We have seen that for Blake truth is a matter of opinion or faith and so 'a firm perswasion that a thing is so' may well 'make it so'. Seeing what the lamb and the tiger are in this kind of way, and the living consequences of so seeing them, are all the work of the human mind.

The Little Black Boy
The first stanza with its contrast of

> White as an angel is the English child,
> But I am black, as if bereav'd of light.

shows how any awareness of racial difference tends to slip into an assumption of racial superiority or inferiority. In the light of eternity, where 'God does live,' the difference between black and white 'Is but a cloud' obscuring the truth that both are equal 'When I from black and he from white cloud free'.

Blake may also be hinting that because the blacks have suffered more in the material world than the whites have, and at the hands of the whites, they may be better able 'the heat to bear' of God's 'love & care'. God's love, the innocent light of eternity in which both children will 'like lambs rejoice', illuminates but it also burns. Those who have caused suffering have more to fear from its being revealed than do those who have borne it. Hence the tender concern that the black child seems to feel in the last stanza to 'shade' the white child 'from the heat, till he can bear/To lean in joy upon our father's knee'. The last illustration seems to show the black boy presenting the white child to God, shown in his loving guise as Jesus the good shepherd.

The Blossom
The Sick Rose (*Songs of Experience*)

The repeated use of 'Near my bosom' as a resting place or 'cradle' for the birds suggests that the child who speaks in 'The Blossom' is a girl, feeling motherly concern for these wild creatures. She speaks of the 'happy Blossom' as if it, too, felt concern for them, and so the poem unites birds, plants, and human beings together in harmony. The robin is not necessarily 'sobbing' for sorrow (the child of 'Introduction' had 'wept with joy' and one of the 'Proverbs of Hell' says that 'Excess of sorrow laughs. Excess of joy weeps') but that is probably the case, for its feelings would then balance those of the 'Merry, Merry Sparrow' in the first stanza, and so emphasise the harmonising power of the concern being expressed, in that it brings together on equal terms both the happy and the sad.

The connections between 'The Blossom' and 'The Sick Rose' are looser than is usual in these contrary pairings but they are there. Instead of the *Innocence* vision of natural harmony *Experience* sees nature as destructively divided against itself, as the worm, a traditional emblem of mortality, undermines the health of the rose. But this state of division is no more 'true' or 'natural' than is the state of harmony presented in 'The Blossom', for both are mental images of nature. The simple contrast is one of Blake's 'apparent surfaces' which must be melted away to reveal what it hides.

'The Sick Rose' is set in that fallen world of experience whose principles are defined in 'Introduction' and 'Earth's Answer'. Specifically, this poem picks up and develops the theme of how the secrecy and shame with which conventional morality tries to restrain the sexual impulse make love itself sick. It is not love as such that destroys the life of the rose but a particular kind of love, one that is secretive instead of open and unashamed. Note how skilfully Blake uses the echoes in the consonant sounds to bind these words together:

> And his *dark secret love*
> *Does thy life destroy.*

The rose is not even an innocent victim: that the devious worm 'Has found out' her 'bed/Of crimson joy' suggests that she had tried to hide it, to conceal (even from herself?) that she might enjoy feeding her sexual appetite (worms and roses are commonly used as respectively male and female sexual symbols). 'The Sick Rose' is almost less a contrary of 'The Blossom' than an indication of the processes which corrupt the innocence portrayed in it.

The Chimney Sweeper
The Chimney Sweeper (*Songs of Experience*)

In Blake's time chimneys were swept by sending small children (both boys and girls, though Blake's poems deal only with boys) to climb up them and clean them out by hand. From as young an age as four or five children would do this work for about seven years, by which time they were too big to crawl through what could be extremely narrow spaces. Or too broken in health, for the practice was not just temporarily cruel: growing bodies were stunted and deformed, and such delicate parts as the lungs, eyes, and developing sexual organs could all be permanently affected by the soot. In 1788, just one year before *Songs of Innocence*, 'An Act for the better regulation of chimney sweepers, and their Apprentices' was passed by Parliament. It was a weak law and difficult to enforce, and its ineffectiveness must have been apparent to any concerned person by the time that Blake composed the second 'Chimney Sweeper'. Not until as late as 1875, however, was it finally made illegal to send children up chimneys.

A carefree child is a natural symbol of innocence, just as a child abused and exploited makes a natural symbol of innocence betrayed or perverted, especially when that exploitation serves the end of financial gain for adults. But Blake is also writing about a specific social problem, and doing so in specific terms. When the *Innocence* sweep says his father 'sold' him he speaks the plain truth: master sweeps paid from 20 shillings to five guineas to the parents or guardians of the children whom they took as 'apprentices'. When he says 'in soot I sleep' it is no metaphor: the children collected the soot that they cleaned up in bags which they often had to store in their lodgings. Even Tom Dacre's nightmare of 'thousands of sweepers . . . lock'd up in coffins of black' might be all too real to a child who could be trapped in a lightless, airless shaft as little as nine inches wide. Even in this *Innocence* poem the indictment of a mercenary, uncaring society is detailed and complete. Its force is not lessened by the fact that the poem also celebrates the power of the imagination, even in such circumstances, to envisage happiness and warmth with such intensity that they become real. It is a fact and not an illusion that 'Tho' the morning was cold, Tom was happy & warm'.

That does not, of course, excuse the circumstances, a fact that is implicit in the *Innocence* poem and is made explicit by the child himself in the *Experience* one:

> 'And because I am happy & dance & sing,
> They think they have done me no injury.'

So the two poems largely cover the same ground as each other. The main difference between them is that in *Innocence* the liberating vision of the Angel shows the reality of the spiritual life and its potential for improving the quality of material life. In *Experience*, however, this is lost behind the hypocritical practices of a church that supports the social and political establishment while being indifferent to the sufferings of the weak and helpless:

> And are gone to praise God & his Priest & King,
> Who make up a heaven of our misery.

The Little Boy Lost
The Little Boy Found
A Little Boy Lost (*Songs of Experience*)
The two *Innocence* poems combine to present the relationship of parent and child as one of mutual care, trust, and affection. The boy is not deserted by his father but is led away from him by a will-o'-the-wisp, a phosphorescent light sometimes seen over marshy ground ('the lonely fen' in which the poems are set). The God who comes to the boy's aid is no remote and awesome being but rather the kindly father promised in the chimney sweeper's dream, an intimate friend and helper who kisses him and takes him by the hand.

The God served by the Priest of 'A Little Boy Lost' is very different: he is cruel – the boy is burned 'in a holy place,/Where many had been burn'd before' – and remote – the Priest's talk about 'our most holy Mystery' which is beyond the 'reason' of a mere child. In 'To Nobodaddy' (which is only three pages away from the first draft of 'A Little Boy Lost' in Blake's manuscript notebook) after the

'Father of Jealousy' has hidden himself 'in clouds/From every searching Eye' the poet asks:

> Why darkness & obscurity
> In all thy words & laws,
> That none dare eat the fruit but from
> The wily serpents jaws?

The serpent symbolises the clergy of the conventional church.
Presenting themselves as the only true interpreters of God's 'words &
laws' they create an aura of 'holy Mystery' in order to keep people in
ignorance, and so in subjection. Note that the burning of the boy is
the Priest's doing. The boy is no more betrayed by his parents than is
his counterpart in *Songs of Innocence*, and we are twice told that 'The
weeping parents wept in vain.' They do not approve of what is done,
much less collaborate in it, but they are as helpless as their child
is.

The innocent reasoning by which the boy offends the Priest's
'trembling zeal' expresses Blake's view of what true religious feeling
is. In the fourth chapter of *Jerusalem* Blake wrote:

> the Worship of God is honouring his gifts
> In other men: & loving the greatest men best, each according
> To his Genius: which is the Holy Ghost in Man; there is no other
> God than that God who is the intellectual fountain of Humanity.

In *The Everlasting Gospel* (written about 1818) Blake expresses the
same idea with more dramatic directness:

> God wants not Man to Humble himself . . . .
> This is the Race that Jesus ran:
> Humble to God, haughty to Man . . .
> And when he Humbled himself to God,
> Then descended the Cruel Rod.
> 'If thou humblest thyself, thou humblest me;
> Thou also dwell'st in Eternity.
> Thou art a Man, God is no more,
> Thy own humanity learn to adore,
> For that is my Spirit of Life.'

Blake derived this view from reasoning hinted at in the third and
fourth lines of 'A Little Boy Lost' where the child says that it is not
'possible to Thought/A greater than itself to know.' The idea is

spelled out in a marginal annotation written around 1789 in Blake's copy of Swedenborg's *Wisdom of Angels Concerning Divine Love and Divine Wisdom* (English translation 1788). Alongside Swedenborg's observation that 'In all the Heavens there is no other idea of God than that of a Man' Blake wrote:

Man can have no idea of any thing greater than Man, as a cup cannot contain more than its capaciousness. But God is a man, not because he is so perciev'd by man, but because he is the creator of man.

Thus the boy cannot conceive of love for God as being different in kind from love for human beings, even from love for himself, in the sense of faith in himself, in the quality of his own humanity. It would have to be love as natural even as that which he might feel for 'the little bird/That picks up crumbs around the door.' Such a personal relationship with God would have no need of priests to control it.

Laughing Song
Like 'The Blossom' this poem shows happy, carefree children in full harmony with all nature. Not only 'Mary and Susan and Emily' but also plants, insects, birds, even the very air, all together 'laugh with the voice of joy'. This is of course a subjective or mental image. The humanising of nature in the children's imaginations is apparent in almost every line. But that does not make the vision less true, rather, it emphasises how completely the children identify themselves with their environment.

A Cradle Song
A lullaby sung by a mother who is, as parents usually are in *Songs of Innocence*, tender, loving, and protective. To assist her own loving care of her child the mother calls upon an 'Angel mild' to ensure sweet dreams, as such an angel does in 'The Chimney Sweeper', and upon that love of God for all humanity that led to his incarnation as Christ, who

> Wept for me, for thee, for all,
> When he was an infant small.

It is important to realise that the mother is not simply being sentimental. 'A Cradle Song' is founded in the same conception of true religious feeling as was discussed in the commentary on 'A Little

Boy Lost' above. A few lines after the passage from *Jerusalem* quoted there we read:

> He who would see the Divinity must see him in his Children,
> One first, in friendship & love, then a Divine Family, & in
>   the midst
> Jesus will appear . . . .

Spiritual love can only come about as a result of human love, and is sustained by it. 'A Cradle Song' shows this in its progression from a mother's love, through an angel's promise of supernatural protection, to the physical expression of God's love in the birth of Christ, whose life then gave a perfect example of human love – 'God becomes as we are, that we may be as he is' (*There is No Natural Religion*, second series).

Blake composed a contrary 'Cradle Song' but it exists only in manuscript and he is not known ever to have etched it for use in *Songs of Experience*. It was probably an early attempt at such countering of a song of innocence and he may have been dissatisfied with it as it does not do much more than parody the earlier poem. Thus the mother still seems to feel personal affection for her child, but now she is suspicious of just what dreams might be passing through its mind:

> O, the cunning wiles that creep
> In thy little heart asleep.
> When thy little heart does wake,
> Then the dreadful lightnings break.

The Divine Image
The Human Abstract (*Songs of Experience*)
It is appropriate that 'The Divine Image' follows 'A Cradle Song' in no fewer than 11 of Blake's 34 different arrangements of *Songs of Innocence*, almost a third of the total. In 'A Cradle Song' the fact that we come to know God by 'honouring his gifts/In other men' is dramatised in a mother's love for her child. In 'The Divine Image' that proposition receives the most explicit statement that it is given anywhere in the *Songs*.

Man's image of God as 'our father dear' rather than as 'old Nobodaddy aloft' ('Let the Brothels of Paris be Opened', written about 1793) is made up out of 'Mercy, Pity, Peace, and Love', virtues which man values and so attributes to any god whom he is prepared to like. In the first book of *Milton* 'the image of God' is one of 'Pity &

Humanity', and in Chapter Three of *Jerusalem* Vala, the goddess of nature, who has seduced man away from the spiritual life, asks:

> 'Does the voice of my Lord call me again? am I pure thro' his
>   Mercy
> And Pity? . . .
> . . . O Mercy, O Divine Humanity!
> O Forgiveness & Pity & Compassion!'

In 'The Divine Image', as in both of those passages, the image of 'Divine Humanity' goes with the image of God, for the qualities invoked are human ones. Anyone who prays to such a god is effectively praying *for* those qualities, for them to be exercised in the world, and so for human beings to exercise them:

> For Mercy has a human heart,
> Pity a human face,
> And Love, the human form divine,
> And Peace, the human dress.

In another of the marginal annotations in his copy of Swedenborg's *Wisdom of Angels* Blake writes:

> Think of a white cloud as being holy, you cannot love it; but think of a holy man within the cloud, love springs up in your thoughts, for to think of holiness distinct from man is impossible to the affections.

In 'A Divine Image', etched about 1794 but never used in any copy of *Songs of Experience*, Blake composed a simple contrary to 'The Divine Image' by pointing out that 'a Human Heart' can also harbour quite different feelings:

> Cruelty has a Human Heart,
> And Jealousy a Human Face;
> Terror the Human Form Divine,
> And Secrecy the Human Dress.

Similarly though more subtly 'The Human Abstract', which replaced 'A Divine Image', begins by pointing out that the positive virtues themselves can be seen to have a negative side:

> Pity would be no more
> If we did not make somebody Poor;

> And Mercy no more could be
> If all were as happy as we.

'And mutual fear brings peace' rather than its being due to any actual desire for it. An organised system of laws and punishments may make fear of the consequences of doing something outweigh the desire to do it. The Piper of *Innocence* already knew such things: 'The Divine Image' twice tells us that those who pray to the healing virtues do so 'in their *distress*'. And Vala in *Jerusalem* knew that pity could not unite those who had not first been divided. Her speech, quoted above, continues:

> 'If I were pure I should never
> Have known Thee: If I were Unpolluted I should never have
> Glorified thy Holiness or rejoiced in thy great Salvation.'

This recognition of the mutual dependence of purity and impurity is the true meeting of contraries, not the cynical implication in 'The Human Abstract' that a virtue is invalidated and made hypocritical by the existence alongside of it of that which makes it necessary.

The true hypocrite in 'The Human Abstract' is Urizen, and the true subject of the poem is his church, which separates human beings from real spiritual life and enslaves them to a cold, abstract system. In *The Book of Urizen* (1794) 'He form'd a dividing rule', he tried to order the world, with 'scales to weigh' and 'golden compasses,' but

> he saw
> That no flesh nor spirit could keep
> His iron laws one moment . . . .
> And he wept & he called it Pity,
> And his tears flowed down on the winds.

It is Urizen's 'selfish loves' that knit 'a snare' and spread 'baits' for mankind: his laws threaten punishments for disobedience and offer rewards for obedience, as in 'Introduction' and 'Earth's Answer'. This system is the 'Web, dark & cold,' that is 'stretch'd/From the sorrows of Urizen's soul' in *The Book of Urizen*:

> So twisted the cords, & so knotted
> The meshes, twisted like to the human brain
>
> And all call'd it The Net of Religion.

Its counterpart in 'The Human Abstract' is the tree 'Of Mystery' that grows from the root of 'Humility', or submission to authority. The 'Catterpiller and Fly' (the 'Fly' here is perhaps, as is often the case with Blake's use of the word, a butterfly and so the product of the 'Catterpiller') that 'Feed on the Mystery' are priests. In *The Marriage of Heaven and Hell*:

> As the catterpiller chooses the fairest leaves to lay her eggs on, so the priest lays his curse on the fairest joys.

The carrion-eating Raven that nests in the tree's 'thickest shade' symbolises the fear of death. In *Milton* the main purpose

> of thy Priests & of thy Churches
> Is to impress on men the fear of death, to teach
> Trembling & fear, terror, constriction, abject selfishness.

The last stanza of 'The Human Abstract' emphasises the unnaturalness of all this. 'The Gods of the earth and sea' are natural forces, represented as searching 'thro' Nature to find this Tree', but it only grows 'in the Human Brain.'

The titles of the two poems carry some relevant significances of their own. 'The Divine Image' builds up a solid body of living activity for the human affections to relate to. 'The Human Abstract' (and it is worth noting that in the manuscript drafts it is called 'The Human Image', so that 'Abstract' would seem to have been carefully chosen as a more appropriate word) breaks this felt reality down by trying to organise and control it. In a passage from *Jerusalem* quoted in Section 3.2 Blake writes:

> . . . an Abstract . . . is a Negation
> Not only of the Substance from which it is derived,
> A murderer of its own Body, but also a murderer
> Of every Divine Member: it is the Reasoning Power,
> An Abstract objecting power that Negatives every thing.

In that same first chapter of *Jerusalem* Blake writes:

> Negations are not Contraries: Contraries mutually Exist;
> But Negations Exist Not. Exceptions & Objections & Unbeliefs
> Exist not, nor shall they ever be Organized for ever & ever.

'A Divine Image' is nearer to being a true contrary of 'The Divine

Image' than 'The Human Abstract' is. As 'The Sick Rose' does with 'The Blossom', or 'A Little Boy Lost' with 'The Little Boy Lost' and 'The Little Boy Found', 'The Human Abstract' rather shows how the values of innocence are corrupted in the development of experience, how experience cannot coexist with innocence but must destroy it.

Holy Thursday
Holy Thursday (*Songs of Experience*)
From 1704 to 1877 annual services were held in London for the pupils, governors, and patrons of the city's charity schools. From 1782 these services were held in St Paul's Cathedral because there were so many poor children going to these schools. Contemporary reports speak of as many as 6000 children attending the services, so Blake's reference to 'multitudes' is no exaggeration.

Each of the two observers of the event 'sees' something quite different. Or perhaps there is but one observer, seeing it differently in each case because his knowledge and his feelings (his 'experience') have changed. In *Innocence* the children are 'these flowers of London town! . . . multitudes of lambs,/Thousands of little boys & girls raising their innocent hands.' Their benefactors are 'wise guardians of the poor' who seem to take a place of secondary importance in the poem, as its wording sets them 'Beneath' the children rather than above them. I do not think, as some critics do, that the last line is ironic. The 'pity' that the reader is urged to 'cherish' is not an abstract concept or a hypocritical pretence but a practical virtue, embodied in 'the aged men' and practised on the 'multitudes of lambs'. It is pity as it is understood in 'The Divine Image', which follows 'Holy Thursday' in four copies of *Songs of Innocence* and precedes it in no fewer than 12.

Nor do I think it can be doubted that this pity is being beneficially practised. In three copies of *Songs of Innocence* 'Holy Thursday' is directly juxtaposed with 'The Chimney Sweeper'. In two of those three copies 'The Divine Image' is added to them, and in two further copies 'The Divine Image', 'The Chimney Sweeper', 'Holy Thursday', and 'The Lamb' are grouped together. A direct comparison with 'The Chimney Sweeper' would show the consequences for all too many children of not being looked after as the ones in 'Holy Thursday' are. Specifically, one of the happy aspects of the liberating dream in 'The Chimney Sweeper' is that in it the children are cleansed of the soot and grime that, in reality, always clung to them. They 'wash in a river, and shine in the Sun./Then naked & white . . . They rise upon clouds and sport in the wind'. In the first line of 'Holy Thursday' we read about the children's 'innocent faces *clean*,' which may not mean much to us but in Blake's time, and in the context that he sometimes devised for the poem, could be an important practical sign that they are not being neglected.

But the *Experience* 'Holy Thursday' looks away from these children to all of those others who are being neglected and deprived, 'Babes reduc'd to misery . . . And so many children poor'. Moreover, in 'Fed with cold and usurous hand' it casts doubt upon the motives of those who do offer some help. 'Usury' is the technical term for lending money and charging interest on the loan. The speaker is suggesting that the guardians expect some return on their investment of charity: perhaps just such a public display of gratitude as the service in St Paul's could be said to be; perhaps the raising up of a docile and servile workforce. The last stanza shows that the world of innocence is not entirely a closed book to experience, even if it is but a distant dream, as the speaker thinks of a land which would offer peace and plenty for all whether 'the sun does shine' or 'the rain does fall,' a place utterly unlike the 'land of poverty' that he actually sees around him, where 'It is eternal winter'.

Night
The first three stanzas speak of the loving care, the 'blessing/And joy without ceasing,' that the guardian 'angels bright' of innocence are always ready to 'pour', on all life – human, animal, and even vegetable:

> On each bud and blossom,
> And each sleeping bosom.

The nests of the innocent are 'thoughtless' in stanza three because 'The Good . . . Think not for themselves' (from 'Motto to the Songs of Innocence & of Experience', written in 1793 but not used in the published work). They have no need to do so because the angels, the protective ministers of love, 'keep them all from harm.'

This does not mean that suffering and death are excluded, for they have a very real presence in the last three stanzas, 'When wolves and tygers howl for prey', 'The angels, most heedful,' try to turn them aside, but if they fall then they

> Recieve each mild spirit,
> New worlds to inherit.

They take the spirits of both predators and victims into heaven on equal terms, a heaven where 'meekness' can tame 'Wrath' by good example, so that the lion 'can lie down and sleep' beside the 'bleating lamb'. The imagery for this vision of harmony was taken by Blake from the Book of Isaiah, chapter 11, verse 6:

> The wolf also shall dwell with the lamb, and the leopard shall lie down with the kid; and the calf and the young lion and the fatling together; and a little child shall lead them.

Spring
As in 'The Blossom' and 'Laughing Song' a child's delight in nature is expressed through self-identification with it, so that children and animals join together 'Merrily, Merrily, to welcome in the Year.' This reaches a climax in the last stanza, where that refrain changes to 'Merrily, Merrily, *we* welcome in the Year.'

Nurse's Song
Nurse's Song (*Songs of Experience*)
The *Innocence* Nurse is secure and contented and, as with the adults in 'The Ecchoing Green', remembering her own childhood brings her nothing but happiness:

> My heart is at rest within my breast
> And everything else is still.

So she begrudges her charges nothing and easily gives in to their entreaties to be allowed to go on playing 'till the light fades away/And then go home to bed.' She is kind, and feels no real anxiety for herself or for them. But when the *Experience* Nurse remembers her childhood:

> The days of my youth rise fresh in my mind,
> My face turns green and pale.

The children's play reminds her of her own youthful hopes and desires, which presumably have not been realised for she becomes envious and resentful:

> Your spring & your day are wasted in play,
> And your winter and night in disguise.

She seems to be suggesting that a childhood spent in play tends to lead to unreality and deceitfulness in later life, but this, like her fussy concern to protect the children from 'the dews of night', is an excuse for repressing them.

Her jealousy and fear ('green and pale' suggests those two emotions) may also be aroused by her awareness of the children's awakening sexuality. The distinction between 'the voices of children are heard on the green/And whisp'rings are in the dale' could imply that the older children are slipping away from the younger ones to flirt with each other. The manuscript draft originally had 'The desires of youth' instead of 'The days of my youth' rising 'fresh in my mind'. A cancelled line in the unused contrary of 'A Cradle Song' made it fairly clear that one of the things that worried the mother as she sat over her sleeping child was the thought that its dreams might be sexual:

> Sweet Babe, in thy face
> Soft desires I can trace
> Secret joys & secret smiles
> Such as burning youth beguiles.

Blake changed that last line to the less pointed 'Little pretty infant wiles.' Sexual play amongst children might well inspire real fear in a young adult charged with looking after them, fear mixed with guilt at having done such things herself. That mixture would then explain both the over-anxious care and the sharp rebuke that we find in the second stanza.

Infant Joy
Infant Sorrow (*Songs of Experience*)

The dialogue in the first stanza of 'Infant Joy' is obviously fanciful as a baby 'but two days old' would not be able to talk, but Blake probably wants to show that the bond of love and sympathy between mother and child is such that they can effectively communicate with each other anyway. The child is an embodiment of happiness – 'I happy am,/Joy is my name' – and inspires that same feeling in the mother. In 'Infant Sorrow' the child is a cause of pain to its parents – 'My mother groan'd! my father wept' – and seems to feel frightened and threatened by 'the dangerous world' in which it is 'Helpless, naked,' its existence already a process of 'Struggling' and 'Striving'. The second stanza shows selfish calculation already at work in this infant, as it plays one parent off against the other:

> Struggling in my father's hands,
> . . . I thought best
> To sulk upon my mother's breast.

The illustration shows a naked male child on a bed, his arms reaching up and out as his mother bends towards him, his father nowhere in sight. In the first draft the poem continued for another six stanzas, all much revised in the manuscript before they were abandoned, in which Blake developed this theme of rivalry between father and son.

A Dream
The Angel (*Songs of Experience*)
'A Dream' presents the work of one of those angels of innocence who watch over the sleep of children and bring them sweet dreams. The imagery of this particular dream shows the protective love and security that guard even the least of the dwellers in innocence in action. An ant ('Emmet') loses its way in the night, but is found and guided safely home to its children by a glow-worm and a beetle.

The dreaming girl in 'The Angel' is also 'Guarded by an Angel mild', but though he is gentle and comforting – 'And he wip'd my tears away' – he is unable to charm away her sorrow: 'Witless woe was ne'er beguil'd!' Her woe is 'Witless' because she does not understand its cause, any more than she understands the dream that arises from it. But both her lack of understanding and the Angel's inability to comfort her are probably due to her concealing her real feelings:

> And I wept both day and night,
> And hid from him my heart's delight.

In the illustration she extends one arm and hand to push the Angel away. She actually fears the Angel and his attentions, and deliberately strengthens those fears as a defence against him, so that when he 'came again:/I was arm'd, he came in vain'.

Her dream of being 'a maiden Queen' probably expresses fear of sexual experience and a desire to avoid it by clinging to an artificial impression of innocence. The illustration shows her as a physically mature young woman, her breasts even emphasised by the overpainting in some copies, and not a child. She will not let her guardian angel help her through the transition from innocence to experience because she does not want to make that transition. Like his counterparts in *Songs of Innocence* this angel of experience would help his charge through the pains and pleasures of life, but fear of the unknown makes her resist him until it is too late:

> For the time of youth was fled,
> And grey hairs were on my head

On Another's Sorrow

Only two copies of *Songs of Innocence* alone are concluded by this poem, but it stands at the end of the *Innocence* sequence in ten copies of the combined *Songs of Innocence and of Experience*. In that context it comes as a final statement of the central faith of innocence, before the harsher vision of experience shows what human beings all too often do to that vision.

The poem restates the importance of the ability to empathise with others, to feel for and with them so completely that their feelings become as your own, and it does so by simply assuming that it is impossible *not* so to feel. The point is that in the state of innocence it *is* impossible to 'see another's woe,/And not be in sorrow too'. Thus moved, the innocent being will inevitably try to help:

> Can I see another's grief,
> And not seek for kind relief?

'The Divine Image' tells us that the ability to feel and to act like this is godlike, and 'On Another's Sorrow' tells us that God became human in order to share in human sorrow:

> He becomes a man of woe;
> He doth feel the sorrow too.

By sharing it God shows us how to rise above it, giving 'to us his joy/That our grief he may destroy'. This is *Innocence*'s last example of how 'God becomes as we are, that we may be as he is.'

4.3 SONGS OF EXPERIENCE

Introduction
Earth's Answer

Taken together these two poems complement the 'Introduction' to *Songs of Innocence*. When *Songs of Innocence* ends with 'On Another's Sorrow' they also counter that poem's assumption of an essential equality between human beings and their god. The god of these poems seeks to bind human beings in subjection to him.

The Clod and the Pebble

Fifteen of the 24 copies of *Songs of Experience* for which we know Blake's ordering place 'The Clod and the Pebble' next after 'Introduction' and 'Earth's Answer'. Since those two poems combine to make a real introduction to the sequence this effectively makes 'The

Clod and the Pebble' the first song of experience in more than half of the known copies. This is fitting, for it deals with attitudes towards love, a theme raised in the introductory poems, and does so by presenting two contrary views, thereby repeating within itself the broader scheme of *Songs of Innocence and of Experience* as a whole.

The 'little Clod of Clay' gives a positive view of love as a state which, without any taint of self-interest, works to make the best of the conditions of life. Love 'for another gives its ease,' as God had done in 'On Another's Sorrow', 'And builds a Heaven in Hell's despair.' But to the 'Pebble of the brook' love is only a hypocritically evasive name for self-interest, which seeks 'To bind another to Its delight,' and so serves to make things worse: 'And builds a Hell in Heaven's despite.' The conflict is only stated in the poem, not resolved. That the Clod is 'Trodden with the cattle's feet' should not be taken as implying that its view is false or unrealistic. That fate is but one of those harsh facts of life which, if not made more bearable by love, make life equivalent to 'Hell's despair.'

In *The Book of Thel* another 'Clod of Clay' appears as an embodiment of a mother's self-sacrificing love for her child. She tells Thel, a virginal innocent on the edge of experience but fearing and resisting it as the dreaming girl of 'The Angel' does, that 'we live not for ourselves', echoing an earlier statement in the poem that 'Every thing that lives/Lives not alone nor for itself.' Thel is afraid that she might 'only live to be at death the food of worms', but is told:

> Then if thou art the food of worms, O virgin of the skies,
> How great thy use, how great thy blessing!

Change, suffering, even death are all necessary conditions of life. If life is to be more than mere existence we must make the best of it rather than merely endure it. The motherly Clod tells Thel:

> But how this is, sweet maid, I know not, and I cannot know;
> I ponder, and I cannot ponder; yet I live and love.

In this light the Clod in 'The Clod and the Pebble' could be seen as embodying a healthy, positive attitude towards life – the innocent attitude, in fact – while the Pebble's cynical 'realism' is not just a denial of love, it is an attempt to deny life itself, to deny that it can have meaning. That it is 'a Pebble of the brook' may mean that it is trapped in the waters of materialism, a recurrent symbol in Blake. They appear in 'Introduction' as 'The wat'ry shore' which Urizen wants the fallen 'Earth' ('Clod of Clay'?) to accept, and are there associated with the stars of Urizenic reasoning in 'The starry floor'. Certainly the Clod's view of what love *is* corresponds to what Earth wants it to be, just as the Pebble's view corresponds to what the 'Father of Jealousy' actually offers her. There is also a relevant unpublished manuscript poem in Blake's notebook under the title of 'How to know Love from Deceit':

> Love to faults is always blind,
> Always is to joy inclin'd,
> Lawless, wing'd, & unconfin'd,
> And breaks all chains from every mind.
>
> Deceit to secresy confin'd,
> Lawful, cautious, & refin'd;
> To every thing but interest blind
> And forges fetters for the mind.

Holy Thursday
Contrary of 'Holy Thursday' in *Songs of Innocence*.

The Little Girl Lost
The Little Girl Found
These two poems were originally in *Songs of Innocence* but have been transferred to *Experience* in all but one copy of the combined sequence. Together they tell a story which is loosely similar to that of 'The Little Boy Lost' and 'The Little Boy Found' but more complex, in that it is a story of a child successfully growing up and becoming independent of her parents. Blake probably relocated the poems because they thus deal with a transition from innocence to experience. Their original status as songs of innocence is apparent from several features of the poems: the transition is successfully accomplished; the parents accept it when they see that she is happy; and the independent state that is achieved looks more like a higher kind of innocence than it does like experience as it is presented elsewhere in the *Songs* (there is a striking resemblance to the 'New worlds' to be inherited by 'each mild spirit' in 'Night').

'The Little Girl Lost' opens by presenting this story as a 'prophetic' vision of a 'futurity' in which 'the earth' rises from her 'sleep' and seeks 'For her maker meek'. The imagery certainly is prophetic of 'Introduction' and 'Earth's Answer', where a fallen 'Earth' lies in bondage to a tyrant god who has usurped the place of a gentle and caring one. It may be significant that Lyca comes from 'the southern clime'. In Blake's developed symbolism the south is the compass-point assigned to Urizen, and Lyca's story could be read as an idealised account of Earth's freeing herself from his rule. Certainly Urizen's 'tygers' appear amongst 'the beasts of prey' who 'View'd the maid asleep', and who then 'play/Round her as she lay,' tamed, like their counterparts in 'Night', by this example of 'meekness'. In four copies of *Songs of Experience* 'The Tyger' either precedes or follows these poems and perhaps such an example would tame it as well, converting it to its contrary of 'The Lamb'? When Lyca's parents meet 'A couching lion' in 'The Little Girl Found' they are frightened at first:

> But their fears allay
> When he licks their hands,
> And silent by them stands.

They see the lion now as 'A Spirit arm'd in gold', which leads them to where 'their sleeping child' lies 'Among tygers wild', and there 'To this day they dwell'. Having faced up to the human potential for violent passion, which is one of the things symbolised by these animals, they can come to terms with it:

> Nor fear the wolvish howl
> Nor the lions' growl.

The innocent child provides an example of how this may be brought about, and the 'innocent' features of the poems, listed above, fall into place in their new context: this is what human beings might make even of the state of experience if they will but think, and feel, and act rightly.

The Chimney Sweeper
Contrary of 'The Chimney Sweeper' in *Songs of Innocence*.

Nurse's Song
Contrary of 'Nurse's Song' in *Songs of Innocence*.

The Sick Rose
Contrary of 'The Blossom' in *Songs of Innocence*.

The Fly
The mental processes of the speaker of this poem are characterised by that partial and self-centred vision typical of the state of expe-

rience. Having unthinkingly killed a fly he is briefly moved to reflect that his own hold on life may be as precarious as that of the insect. One day 'some blind hand', an image of a remote and mysterious god, shall swat him, too. The lives of man and fly are equal on the most basic level, they both 'dance,/And drink, & sing,' and only the capacity for thought raises human life higher than that. Life without thought 'is death', and since he has just been 'thoughtless' his life is worth no more than a fly's, and his death would be no more important.

That sounds as if the speaker's consciousness transcends the limitations of experience, but his way of thinking is not Blake's. The speaker certainly feels guilty about having killed the fly, and the manuscript draft of the poem originally had 'guilty' instead of 'thoughtless' in the first stanza, but all it seems to lead to is his feeling sorry for himself. Blake may have substituted 'thoughtless' for 'guilty' precisely to reduce the impression of the speaker's compassion for the fly. also, the speaker's reasoning consistently assumes that human life is, or at least ought to be, more important than insect life, whereas truly innocent vision knows that 'every thing that lives is Holy' (*The Marriage of Heaven and Hell*). 'A Dream' in *Songs of Innocence* (and 'The Angel', the contrary of that poem, now follows 'The Fly') treats an ant, a glow-worm, and a beetle as the spiritual equals of human beings. More specifically, compare the speaker's attitude with the one expressed in these lines from the first book of *Milton*:

Seest thou the little winged fly, smaller than a grain of sand?
It has a heart like thee, a brain open to heaven & hell,
Withinside wondrous & expansive: its gates are not clos'd:
I hope thine are not: hence it clothes itself in rich array:
Hence thou art cloth'd with human beauty, O thou mortal man.

The illustration deserves some comment, if only because it seems to have so little to do with the poem. It shows a mother or nurse holding a little boy's arms as she apparently teaches him to walk. Behind them a girl, somewhat older than the boy, knocks a shuttle-cock about with a racket. At first glance it all seems innocuous enough, but they are surrounded by the bare trees that are so common in the *Experience* plates, a fact which makes it possible to interpret this as an image of sterile conditioning rather than one of happy childhood. The boy seems rather old to be being taught to walk, and it could be that he is being controlled and not helped. The girl stands apart, her back turned towards her companions and the viewer, and her game could be thought lonely and pointless, especially since it really calls for a second player. The children are acquiring the habits of a regimented (and so essentially 'thoughtless') existence. Potential fly-swatters both!

The Angel
Contrary of 'A Dream' in *Songs of Innocence*.

The Tyger
Contrary of 'The Lamb' in *Songs of Innocence*.

My Pretty Rose Tree
Ah! Sun-flower
The Lilly
Blake etched these three short poems together on a single plate. He may well have done so simply for reasons of convenience, but there are interesting connections to be made between them and the fact that they do occupy the same page invites us to make those connections.

'My Pretty Rose Tree' is often interpreted as an allegorical account of a wife's jealousy – sometimes to the accompaniment of ingenious attempts to relate it to hypothetical circumstances in Blake's own life. The speaker virtuously rejects the offer of 'Such a flower as May never bore' in favour of fidelity to his own 'Pretty Rose-tree,' only to discover that she reacts with anger and resentment as if he had taken the offer anyway, 'And her thorns were my only delight.' In the second poem the sunflower, by which Blake means the heliotrope which turns its face to follow the sun across the sky, is being used as a symbol of human aspiration towards the spiritual, 'that sweet golden clime/Where the traveller's journey is done' – death, or the afterlife. The Youth and the Virgin of the second stanza, dissatisfied with the imperfections of material existence (like the sunflower they are 'weary of time'), pine for a pure perfection that will only be available when they have escaped from bondage to mortal flesh. 'The Lilly' is a symbol of pure love, with nothing to 'stain her beauty bright', unlike the Rose who 'puts forth a thorn' to protect herself.

'Ah! Sun-flower' is the crucial poem in this triptych. It presents aspiration away from the material and towards the spiritual in its negative form: less a desire to transcend the limitations of physical existence than a desire simply to escape them. It is spiritual aspiration perverted into a kind of death wish. The Youth and the Virgin can be seen as believers in that error that Blake had attacked in *The Marriage of Heaven and Hell*, the belief 'That Man has two real existing principles: Viz: a Body & a Soul.' Immortality for them is something that they can only achieve when their mortal parts have died and they can 'Arise from their graves' and go to a better, purer world. It sounds suspiciously like the 'heaven' of conventional religious teaching.

The heroine of *The Book of Thel* is another such timid virgin, with a 'white veil' to correspond to this one's being 'shrouded in snow'. Thel has an imaginative vision of 'her own grave plot' from which she hears a 'voice of sorrow' complaining about the nature of bodily life, especially its attributes of sexuality and mortality. She retreats from this vision, running away back to her home in 'the vales of Har', which represent a state of self-love. The snowy shroud of the Virgin in 'Ah! Sun-flower' suggests a similar state of frozen sterility.

If we read 'Ah! Sun-flower' in this way then it provides a context which might make us suspect that stainless purity of 'The Lilly'. Experience teaches us that nothing really is that pure, in the sense of simple or unmixed: roses have thorns as well as blossoms, and even 'The humble Sheep' will fight if it is aroused. The kind of love in which 'the Lilly white shall . . . delight' could be seen as evasive, an idealistic oversimplification of the complexities of reality. The lily in the design that accompanies the poem does not stand proudly up, it droops towards the ground as if pining away like the Youth described above it. In Blake's symbolism the rose is usually emblematic of love and the lily of innocence. When the two are united together an ideal state exists, but 'The Lilly' seems to be distinguishing and separating them, and so tending to promote a false view of what either really is.

If we now look again at 'My Pretty Rose Tree', we could say that the speaker in that poem is misled by a false view of love and by an apparent belief that human responses can be rationally predictable, for he assumes that faithfulness will be rewarded. It may even be that hc is only faithful *because* he expects to be rewarded. Such beliefs can be seen as a false and shallow kind of idealism. Also, although the rose tree's jealousy is a selfish and possessive emotion he, too, is possessive, talking of '*my* Pretty Rose-tree' and '*my* Rose'. He expects his fidelity and his readiness 'To tend her by day and by night' to be met with gratitude and devotion from his rose, and he is upset when this does not happen. His feelings are self-centred and unrealistic, as is suggested by his apparent surprise and disturbance at the discovery that roses have thorns as well as blossoms. At the foot of the page 'The Lilly' opens by noting that they inevitably do, even if the tone of that poem is then one of regret that this should be so.

Perhaps the regret is for the fact that love, or even existence itself, cannot be as pure and simple in the world of experience as it is in that of innocence. This lily may droop because experience, where it now finds itself, is not the right kind of environment for its healthy growth. Innocence and experience are incompatible.

The Garden of Love

An attack on restrictive, negative morality. The 'many sweet flowers' that grow in the garden of love are 'joys & desires', those passionate movements of the human spirit that make up that 'Energy' which 'is Eternal Delight' in life. Conventional morality, figured in the Chapel with its 'shut' gates and the words '"Thou shalt not" writ over the door', seeks to control these 'joys & desires' and so kills them. In *The Marriage of Heaven and Hell* Blake had written:

> Those who restrain desire, do so because theirs is weak enough to be restrained; and the restrainer or reason usurps its place & governs the unwilling.
> And being restrain'd, it by degrees becomes passive, till it is only the shadow of desire.

This process is the death of vital, active life because, as we have already seen, for Blake the reason alone cannot generate new ideas, new life. Reading on in the *Marriage* from the passage just quoted we find Blake arguing that Christ prayed 'to the Father to send the comforter, or Desire, that Reason might have new Ideas to build on'.

Another consequence of this attempt to restrain 'the unwilling' is the growth of that shameful secrecy about sexual love that we have seen in 'Introduction' and 'Earth's Answer' and which lies behind 'The Sick Rose'. In five copies of *Songs of Experience* 'The Sick Rose' either precedes or follows 'The Garden of Love'.

The design for the poem visually reinforces these suggestions of the deadening nature of restraint upon desire. At the top of the page a boy, a girl, and a priest kneel in prayer at the edge of an open grave. The text of the poem, intertwined with roots and worms, is placed under, and so, effectively, buried *in* this grave.

The Little Vagabond

The child who speaks in this poem is experienced enough to be fully aware of the difference between the coldness and dullness of a church and the 'healthy & pleasant & warm' atmosphere of an ale-house, but innocent enough to wonder why, if God is 'pleasant and happy', the conditions under which he is worshipped cannot be so as well. The implication of this for the reader is that there is a difference between the real nature of God and the manner in which 'the Parson' and his like have ordained that people should think of him. Blake may also be implying that the practices of the church do not meet people's real needs. Note that 'healthy' is placed first amongst the adjectives used to describe the ale-house in stanza one, while in stanza three the fact that 'modest dame Lurch . . . is always at Church' has not kept her from having 'bandy children'. They are 'bandy' because they suffer from rickets, a disease caused by dietary deficiency. That they suffer from 'fasting' in addition to this suggests that she deliberately makes them go short of food, perhaps in a misguided attempt to teach them the 'virtues' of self-restraint and contempt for the appetites of the flesh. She beats them with a 'birch' for the same reason. Both practices would be approved and promoted by the church of this poem.

London

An extraordinarily compressed and powerful denunciation of the inequities of Blake's society, inequities which, in the first half of the poem, are presented as the consequences of the regimentation of people's lives within the social system. A charter is a legal document granting specified rights or privileges to specified individuals or classes of people. It states what they are allowed to do, and so necessarily implies, and may explicitly state, what they are not allowed to do. It is a prohibition as well as a licence, and so 'charter'd' in the first stanza is related to 'every ban' in the second. The basic meaning of 'ban', still current in Blake's time, was 'curse'. As such it fits well with 'every cry of every Man' and 'every Infant's cry of fear' in the second stanza, and with 'the youthful Harlot's curse' in the fourth. But it also meant a prohibition, and moreover had the technical meaning of an official public proclamation of something – a law, or a sentence upon someone. 'Charter'd' also has a relevant secondary meaning, in that a charter could be a legal document setting out details of the ownership of landed property. Property rights, laws, curses, prohibitions, such are 'The mind-forg'd manacles' that hold the social system together. They are 'mind-forg'd' because they have been made up, they are not natural, and they are 'manacles' because they only work by denying freedom of action to the individuals who make up society. As in 'The Human Abstract', the next poem in nine copies of *Songs of Experience*, 'mutual fear brings peace'.

The second half of the poem explores the living consequences of this state of affairs. The chimney sweeper is, as the two poems about him have already shown us, an example of the callous exploitation of child labour. The church seems to be aware of his plight, even to be appalled by it, but does not seem to do anything to alleviate it. Perhaps the church is 'black'ning' both literally, under the pall of smoke and soot associated with that plight, and metaphorically, its standing in society tarnished by its shameful inability or unwillingness to act. The soldier is 'hapless', or luckless, because he can be seen as both an agent and a victim of repression: the blood he is called upon to shed in the service of his monarch is as likely to be his own as anyone else's. That is why it is his own 'sigh' that 'Runs in blood down Palace walls.'

In this context we are probably to see the 'youthful Harlot' of the last stanza as having been forced into prostitution by sheer economic necessity. We are certainly to see prostitution itself as a consequence of that conventional morality which tries to contain and control sexual desire and so makes prostitution inevitable. One of the 'Proverbs of Hell' maintains that 'Prisons are built with stones of Law, Brothels with bricks of Religion.' The kind of moral argument that Blake is thinking of can be exemplified by a passage in the preamble to the marriage service in the Church of England's *Book of Common Prayer* which states that one of the reasons why marriage was ordained was

to avoid fornication; that such persons as have not the gift of continency might marry, and keep themselves undefiled members of Christ's body.

The Harlot's 'curse' may be venereal disease, transmitted by her to her clients and by them to their respectable wives and children, so making the marriage bed a 'Marriage hearse.'

Two pages away from the first draft of 'London' in his manuscript notebook Blake wrote these four lines under the title 'An Ancient Proverb':

Remove away that black'ning church:
Remove away that marriage hearse:
Remove away that man of blood:
You'll quite remove the ancient curse.

Four pages away from the draft he wrote this:

Why should I care for the men of thames,
Or the cheating waves of charter'd streams,
Or shrink at the little blasts of fear
That the hireling blows into my ear?

> Tho' born on the cheating banks of Thames,
> Tho' his waters bathed my infant limbs,
> The Ohio shall wash his stains from me:
> I was born a slave, but I go to be free.

The European Romantics thought of revolutionary America as a country of achieved liberty, a New World where the outworn conventions of the Old had been shaken off (see Blake's *America, a Prophecy*). In terms reminiscent of 'London' these lines set the Ohio river, flowing through a land of the 'free', against the 'charter'd streams' of the Thames, alongside which 'the hireling' speaks words 'of fear' and men are born to slavery.

The Human Abstract
Contrary of 'The Divine Image' in *Songs of Innocence*.

Infant Sorrow
Contrary of 'Infant Joy' in *Songs of Innocence*.

A Poison Tree
This is another poem that deals with the attempt to repress personal feelings and shows the harm that this does, whatever those feelings might be – here, the potentially destructive emotion of anger. With his friend the speaker is able to say freely and frankly how he feels, and that feeling is harmlessly discharged:

> I was angry with my friend:
> I told my wrath, my wrath did end.

When he tries to conceal his feelings from his enemy they find no such outlet but instead they work away within him, building up his dislike until it results in the enemy's death. One of the 'Proverbs of Hell' says that 'He who desires but acts not, breeds pestilence', and 'A Poison Tree' dramatises the truth of that observation as the speaker's feelings fester within him. In the second stanza the 'fears' and 'tears' which make his anger grow are probably fear of his enemy, recalling the 'mutual fear' which brings the illusion of 'peace' in 'The Human Abstract', and tears of self-pity over his tormented inner state. He becomes calculatingly deceitful as he tries to lead his enemy into a trap, and is eventually so spiteful and vicious that he can exult in the man's death:

> In the morning glad I see
> My foe outstretch'd beneath the tree.

The first draft of the poem was entitled 'Christian Forbearance', a sardonic comment on the conventional high valuation of restraint and self-effacement, virtues which the poem translates into 'soft deceitful wiles.'

A Little Boy Lost
Contrary of 'The Little Boy Lost' and 'The Little Boy Found' in *Songs of Innocence*.

A Little Girl Lost
Almost certainly intended as a contrary of 'The Little Girl Lost' and 'The Little Girl Found' before those poems were transferred to *Songs of Experience*. Blake's design for the first page of 'The Little Girl Lost' includes a picture of a youth and a physically mature girl embracing under a tree. This does not seem to illustrate anything in 'The Little Girl Lost' and has sometimes been taken as a representation of the 'youthful pair' who 'Met in garden bright' in 'A Little Girl Lost', thus visually relating the two poems to each other.

The first stanza can be taken as an explicit comment by the Bard, with the story that the poem tells beginning in the second stanza. In Blake's etching the style of the lettering in the first stanza is very different from that in the remaining six, an effect usually imitated in modern editions by setting that first stanza in italics. The Bard addresses, '*this indignant page*' to a '*future age*' when, he assumes, sexual love will no longer be '*thought a crime*', and tells the children of that age a story from '*a former time*' when it was thought to be so. That time is, of course, Blake's own.

The 'youthful pair' meet in a garden, in 'the holy light' of 'rising day'. There and then 'On the grass they play . . . And the maiden soon forgot her fear' – they become lovers, in natural innocence and openly, in the light of day, not secretively in the darkness of night (see 'Introduction', 'Earth's Answer', and 'The Sick Rose'). When Ona goes home her stern father, 'his loving look' insincere and hypocritical, invokes the conventional moral law, 'the holy book,' to terrify and subdue her. It is clearly he who thinks of her as 'lost' in the sense of 'fallen into sin'. The design for the poem fills the page with emblems of natural fertility and vitality, which the text blights with this parental and religious condemnation.

The name Ona may not mean anything in particular in this context but Blake did use the name again elsewhere. In his myth Ona is one of the three daughters of Urizen, whom the father of 'A Little Girl Lost' closely resembles. For instance, in both the texts and the illustrations of the Prophetic Books Urizen is consistently associated with the 'holy books' of the laws of his repressive religion, and it is probably he who is named 'The Holy Word' in the 'Introduction' to *Songs of Experience*. Moreover, his daughter Ona symbolises the loins, the sexual parts of the human body (her sisters represent the heart and the head), which would be appropriate for the Ona who awakens to sexuality in 'A Little Girl Lost'.

To Tirzah

This poem is a late addition to the sequence, probably added around 1801, but perhaps as late as 1805. It does not appear in three of the earliest copies of *Songs of Experience*, which end with a page that carries no text, but a symbolic picture representing 'The Regeneration of Earth'. 'To Tirzah' then replaced that plate, concluding the sequence in five copies of the *Songs*. Probably later still Blake moved 'The Schoolboy' and 'The Voice of the Ancient Bard' from *Songs of Innocence* and placed them after 'To Tirzah'.

Blake took the name Tirzah, and some aspects of the role that she plays in his myth, from various references to both a city and a woman of that name in the Old Testament. In his myth she is the daughter of Rahab the harlot, who symbolises sexual licence, but she is herself a prude and so represents sexual repression. One of Blake's many psychological insights was his realisation that prudery and prurience can often go together in the one personality (the *Experience* 'Nurse's) Song' perhaps provides an example, and in 'To Tirzah' we read that 'The Sexes sprung from Shame & Pride'), and so he has Rahab and Tirzah work together to keep mankind preoccupied with the organic rather than the spiritual aspects of life. In Night the Eighth of *The Four Zoas* they weave the natural body – 'webs of torture,/Mantles of despair . . . Veils of ignorance covering from head to feet with a cold web' – to contain the spiritual body. In Book the First of *Milton* they make war on Jerusalem, which represents liberty and imagination, the two things most necessary to human spiritual growth, seeking

> To destroy Jerusalem as a Harlot & her Sons as Reprobates,
> To raise up Mystery the Virgin Harlot, Mother of War,
> Babylon the Great, the Abomination of Desolation.

That is, to make human beings mistrust their individual imaginations, their individual capacities for vision and for independent choice, and to make them submit themselves to external authority instead.

The *Songs of Experience* offer numerous examples of parents behaving thus to their own children, the external authority involved being the parents' own (one such example, 'A Little Girl Lost', where parental authority is supported by the 'Mystery' of religious authority, precedes 'To Tirzah' in the standard order), and the speaker of 'To Tirzah' addresses her as 'Mother of my Mortal part,' the creator of his physical body. As such, she has bound him to organic matter, to the mindless physical cycle of birth and death represented here by 'Generation' and summarised in 'Blow'd in the morn; in evening died'. Blake begins *The Four Zoas* by stating that its subject is in part the story of Urthona, who symbolises the creative imagination of the individual:

> His fall into Divison & his Resurrection to Unity:
> His fall into the Generation of decay & death, & his
> Regeneration by the Resurrection from the dead.

The speaker of 'To Tirzah' has likewise fallen 'into the Generation of decay & death'. He tells his mother that she

> Didst close my Tongue in senseless clay,
> And me to Mortal life betray.

He wishes 'To rise from Generation free' by exercising the 'Divine Vision' of his imagination, and a necessary part of that process is to become self-reliant and self-sufficient, to free himself from undue dependence upon others:

> The Death of Jesus set me free:
> Then what have I to do with thee?

Jesus came to represent for Blake the universal imagination of which the individual creative imagination is a part, and Jesus's life as a man shows the way to a higher kind of life than can be found through concern for material things. The speaker's question echoes Jesus's question (in St John's Gospel, chapter 2, verse 4) to his own mother when she asked a favour of him: 'Woman, what have I to do with thee?'

The illustration shows a naked man reclining on the ground, perhaps dying, supported by two women. An old man bends over him, offering him a jug to drink from. On the old man's clothes are the words 'It is raised a spiritual body'. This is a quotation from St Paul's First Epistle to the Corinthians, chapter 15, verse 44:

> It is sown a natural body; it is raised a spiritual body. There is a natural body, and there is a spiritual body.

This is essentially the same message as was carried by the symbolic picture with which Blake had at first concluded the *Songs*. That had shown a naked male form being carried up into the air by winged cherubs. 'To Tirzah' uses words as well as images to make the message more explicit and precise: the poem is a declaration of the will to achieve independence, to rise above the inadequacies and divisions of the state of experience.

The School Boy
Originally in *Songs of Innocence*, where it remains in 12 copies of the combined sequence. It was transferred to *Songs of Experience* about 1799.

Blake distrusted all formal education. According to Henry Crabb Robinson's records of the conversations he had with him during 1825, Blake would not 'admit that any education should be attempted except of cultivation of the imagination and fine arts.' The poem presents conventional education as a process of deadening the imagination by subjecting it to a 'dreary shower' of learning poured out by bored and uncaring teachers – 'Under a cruel eye outworn'. The pupils are not able to enjoy learning because it does not come as naturally to them as it does to one of the children in the accompanying design. He sits under the open sky in the top of a flourishing vine (perhaps the true 'learning's bower'?), reading a book to himself. Other children in the design are playing with marbles or climbing in the vine, thus being allowed 'their joy in the springing day' instead of spending 'many an anxious hour' in the schoolroom. The last two stanzas argue that such an education cannot be defended on the grounds that it prepares the children for adult life, for 'if buds are nip'd . . . And if the tender plants are strip'd',

> How shall the summer arise in joy,
> Or the summer fruits appear?
> Or how shall we gather what griefs destroy,
> Or bless the mellowing year,
> When the blasts of winter appear?

Their schooling does not so much educate them about the 'sorrow and care's dismay' of experience as inflict it upon them.

The Voice of the Ancient Bard
Like 'The School Boy' this poem was transferred from *Innocence* to *Experience* around 1799. It remains in *Innocence* in 13 copies of the combined *Songs*, and in a fourteenth copy it actually appears twice, once in each section.

62

'The Voice of the Ancient Bard' is generally thought to be a little
later than the other *Songs of Innocence*, perhaps dating from about
1790. That it opens by welcoming 'the opening morn,/Image of truth
new born' may reflect the high hopes that Blake, in common with
other artists and intellectuals of his time, had for the French
Revolution of 1789. Whether that is so or not, the poem certainly
contrasts the supposed wisdom of age and experience with the real
wisdom of youth and innocence. Conventional wisdom is actually
'Folly', and those who follow it 'stumble all night over bones of the
dead,' enslaving themselves to the traditions and habits of a dead
past. One of the 'Proverbs of Hell' urges the reader to 'Drive your
cart and your plow over the bones of the dead' in order to learn and
to create. The 'Image of truth' is the dawn light of 'the opening morn'
in contrast to the darkness of Folly, made up of 'Doubt . . . & clouds
of reason,/Dark disputes & artful teazing.' In 'Auguries of Innocence' we are told that:

> He who shall teach the Child to Doubt
> The rotting Grave shall ne'er get out.

Such are those who 'wish to lead others, when they should be led',
and who do not know that

> He who respects the Infant's faith
> Triumphs over Hell & Death.

Standing where it now does 'The Voice of the Ancient Bard' makes
a fitting conclusion to the sequence. In the 'Introduction' to *Songs of
Experience* the Bard sang of the god of this fallen world holding out
to Earth, for his own purposes, the promise that

> Night is worn,
> And the morn
> Rises from the slumberous mass.

Now, in the last song, the Bard defines the real dawn that would be
able to dispel what 'Earth's Answer' calls 'the darkness dread &
drear' of experience.

4.4 CONCLUSION

At the end of this commentary it is appropriate to repeat a point made at the beginning of it: that neither state of mind, or point of view, is to be thought of as being the 'truth' in any objective, absolute sense. Faced with the pairing of 'Infant Joy' and 'Infant Sorrow' we are not to conclude that one of these contrary versions of the relationship between parents and children is true and the other therefore false, for they are both true. The same child can be all sweetness and smiles one minute, and a struggling fiend the next. And that alternation, that unpredictability, in the behaviour of their children, may cause parents to stop behaving kindly and lovingly, and instead become authoritarian and repressive, like Ona's father in 'A Little Girl Lost'. That in its turn may provoke more of the kind of behaviour shown in 'Infant Sorrow'. I have already suggested that the child in that poem seems to be learning how to play one parent off against the other.

Similarly, in the two 'Holy Thursday' poems we need not think of two observers of the event, each seeing it differently, for it may be more to the point to think of a single observer who is changing his mind about it. The same is true, though in a more complex fashion, of the pairing of 'The Lamb' and 'The Tyger'. If we accept that the poems present subjective reactions and not objective descriptions then it follows that this may be how someone is seeing these creatures rather than how they actually are. If your reactions to other creatures are tender and loving, as those of the child in 'The Lamb' are, then you create around yourself a world full of tenderness and love. But if, as the speaker of 'The Tyger' arguably does, you react to other creatures by recoiling from them in fear and mistrust, feelings bred out of an inability or unwillingness to involve yourself with them or to trust them, then you will create a world full of things that seem to you mysterious and threatening, and will probably feel that you are right to be suspicious of them. In Blake's 1799 letter to Dr Trusler, quoted and discussed in section 3.2 above, he writes that 'As a man is, So he Sees', to which we might add that how a man sees then tends to confirm him in being what he is. Both 'The Lamb' and 'The Tyger' could be being spoken by the same person, feeling, and so seeing, differently under different circumstances. 'The Lilly' points out that 'The humble Sheep' has 'a threat'ning horn' as well as the 'Softest clothing, wooly, bright', mentioned in 'The Lamb', and so it could be dangerous if approached in the wrong manner.

So, whether you see others as approaching you like lambs or like tigers will affect how you react to them, and that may affect how they actually do approach you. We do not know whether the enmity between the speaker and his 'foe' in 'A Poison Tree' was real or imaginary to begin with, but it certainly becomes real as the speaker plots against him. The foe then falls so easily into the speaker's trap because he, too, knows that he has an enemy, and he wants to injure him:

> And my foe beheld it shine,
> And he knew that it was mine,
>
> And into my garden stole
> When the night had veil'd the pole . . . .

That last line has the simple primary meaning of 'when darkness had fallen on the turning world', but another meaning may be latent within the image. In Blake's developed personal symbolism the pole, or polar region, is almost always the North Pole, which is the region of imagination as the South is of reason. It is possible to take the line as meaning something like: 'when the darkness of ignorance and error had clouded the imaginative ability to identify with others and so to appreciate what their true feelings are'. This would not simply mean that, had the enemy been so aware, he would have suspected that the 'apple bright' was the bait in a trap and so not have tried to steal it. Rather, the implication would be that had they both been open and caring – truly 'imaginative' behaviour – with each other, then none of this need have happened.

Blake is not, however, so naïve as to maintain that behaving well towards others will inevitably result in their behaving well in return. In 'Night' in *Songs of Innocence* 'When wolves and tygers howl for prey' the guardian angels

> pitying stand and weep;
> Seeking to drive their thirst away,
> And keep them from the sheep;

but the beasts may still 'rush dreadful' on this easy prey. Only in the ideal 'New worlds' of the last two stanzas is it certain that 'Wrath' will be 'driven away' by 'meekness,' and 'sickness' by 'health'. But 'The Little Girl Found' shows that it is equally possible to choose to behave well without there being any apparent 'cause' for doing so. Lyca's parents are afraid of the lion when they first meet him, and seemingly with good reason, for

> Soon his heavy mane
> Bore them to the ground.
> Then he stalk'd around,
>
> Smelling to his prey . . . .

But then he is gentle with them, behaving as their friend rather than their enemy. They see him as the noble spirit that he is, and 'Gone was all their care.' Gentleness will sometimes be met with violent force, but fear – or even hatred, cruelty, or whatever – can be met with gentleness. There is always a choice.

The *Songs of Innocence and of Experience* are, in part, concerned with the kinds of choices that people make in various circumstances, and how the consequences of those choices then work themselves out. Those consequences are, of course, the experience that confronts, and so often destroys, innocence. At the end of Night the Second of *The Four Zoas* Enion laments that it would be 'an easy thing' to welcome experience if it always came in the form of joy and prosperity, but it does not:

What is the price of Experience? do men buy it for a song?
Or wisdom for a dance in the street? No, it is bought with the price
Of all that a man hath, his house, his wife, his children.
Wisdom is sold in the desolate market where none come to buy,
And in the wither'd field where the farmer plows for bread in vain.

It is understandable enough that the dreaming girl of 'The Angel' might, like Thel, not want to pay such a price, but the price that she pays for trying to avoid the risk of being required to do so is that she avoids life itself.

However attractive a state simple innocence is, it can only be a temporary state. To try to hold on to it beyond its natural term is to deny the possibility of growth. In the margin of one of the pages of the manuscript of *The Four Zoas* Blake wrote:

Unorganiz'd Innocence: An Impossibility.
Innocence dwells with Wisdom, but never with Ignorance.

A purely 'natural' innocence, not founded in any real knowledge of life, is really only ignorance, which is why the harsh facts of experience can so easily, and so devastatingly, shatter it. What that marginal note of Blake's points to is the need to pass through the disappointments of experience to a higher kind of innocence, an insight into life and death attained through honest self-knowledge and through the liberating power of the imagination.

In other words, experience is not to be thought of simply as something that follows innocence and, more or less permanently, replaces it. Experience is but one stage in what should be a continuing process of personal evolution, which may well lead to a renewal of innocence. It is possible to see the relationship between the two 'Holy

Thursday' poems as being the reverse of how it would normally be taken: perhaps the observer's first reaction to what he sees is bitter and angry, but then he begins to see what, for themselves, the children manage to make of it anyway.

The *Songs* also explore another, all too human, reaction to being faced with what *The Four Zoas* calls 'the terrors of the uncertain,' and one that is perhaps worse than simply backing away from experience. This is to try to eliminate the disturbing element of risk by rationally controlling life, as if its uncertainties could thus be limited and contained. It is surely for this reason that in 'The Garden of Love'

> Priests in black gowns were walking their rounds,
> And binding with briars my joys & desires.

In 'Introduction' and 'Earth's Answer' it may be that 'The Holy Word' is afraid that, if 'Earth' is free to choose for herself what she will do, she will not love him as he wishes, and that is why he tries either to buy her affection, or to force it from her. But as men elaborate such rational systems, trying to make them truly effective, they become the Tree of Mystery that we see in 'The Human Abstract', or 'The mind-forg'd manacles' that we hear echoing 'thro' each charter'd street' of 'London'. Conceived of as solutions they have become part of the problem, planting 'tomb-stones where flowers should be'.

So, while it may be inevitable that experience will follow innocence, it is not inevitable that human begins should then stay locked into experience. To progress further may be dauntingly difficult, for all of the reasons so powerfully depicted in *Songs of Experience*, but it is not impossible. The conditions of experience are man-made, and so they can be unmade. Blake's late addition of 'To Tirzah' to the sequence is the addition of an explicit statement that, if the will 'To rise from Generation free' is strong enough, then

> Whate'er is Born of Mortal Birth
> Must be consumed with the Earth . . .

5 BLAKE'S STYLE

5.1 VOICE AND EXPRESSION

Blake uses a wide variety of poetic forms in *Songs of Innocence and of Experience*, and often develops his images in unexpected and devious ways. 'The Lamb' and 'The Tyger' look very different from each other on a modern printed page, let alone on Blake's original plates; and in the third stanza of 'London' a child's cry turns into particles of soot blackening the walls of a church, and then a soldier's sigh becomes bloodstains on the walls of a palace. But the overriding impression left by the poems tends to be one of directness and simplicity of expression. That third stanza of 'London' sets out those two images in just 20 commonplace words.

The apparent simplicity and the concentrated directness of so many of the poems are effects deliberately calculated and worked for by Blake because of their appropriateness to the characters and situations that he is creating. The third stanza of 'The Tyger' ends:

> And when thy heart began to beat,
> What dread hand? & what dread feet?

In the first draft of the poem that question continued for another three lines:

> Could fetch it from the furnace deep
> And in thy horrid ribs dare steep
> In the well of sanguine woe?

In the published text the meaning of the incomplete question is clear enough, and the cancelled lines only spelled it out more. By cutting them Blake removed something that was not strictly necessary and he also gained something for the poem: the question now stands as a broken-off exclamation, which very effectively characterises the speaker's disturbed and excited frame of mind. He starts to frame a question, but then is too overwrought to finish it in a logical and articulate way.

Like many of the *Songs of Experience* 'The Tyger' seems to be trying to imitate, in a realistic manner, the patterns of natural speech. It is one of the characteristics of that sequence that, as a whole, distinguish it from *Songs of Innocence*, where we often find a tendency to stress the lyrical, the songlike, nature of the poetry. This 'musical' effect is achieved in many of the *Songs of Innocence* by using verse forms that are fairly elaborate in their pattern and using them with a regularity that allows that pattern to show itself. The *Songs of Experience*, on the other hand, tend to use simpler forms and to treat them with a freedom that disguises their shape.

5.2 VERSIFICATION

The discussion of metrical form in English poetry is a difficult subject, and one that is surrounded by some controversy, but I shall use a traditional system of analysis by way of the pattern of distribution of 'stresses' or accents amongst the syllables of a line. The basic metrical unit within a line is called a 'foot' and consists of however many syllables the metrical form being used calls for, with the stress falling on whichever syllable the form dictates. Thus an iambic foot, probably the most common metre in English poetry, has two syllables, the first unstressed and the second stressed, as in the word 'allow'. A trochaic foot also has two syllables, but the first is stressed and the second unstressed, as in 'corner'. This system has the advantages of being widely understood and accepted, and it is also the concept of metre that Blake himself would have known and worked from.

'The Lamb' has a stanza form of ten lines, of which four – numbers one, two, nine, and ten – have six syllables arranged as three trochaic feet. The lines making up the central block of six in each stanza have seven syllables in a pattern produced by adding an extra, stressed, syllable at the end of a line that is otherwise like the outer ones. In the third and eighth lines of the second stanza, 'He is callèd by thy name' and 'We are callèd by his name', the word 'callèd' is pronounced as two syllables rather than one, so preserving the metrical pattern. This variation between lines of six syllables and ones of seven, but always with a strictly symmetrical placing of the accents, is very simple, but it is enough to give the effect of musical rhythm to the poem. And to do something more: in normal speech rhythm it might well be the name of God that was stressed in such a remark as 'God bless thee'. In the last two lines of 'The Lamb' the trochaic metre ensures that it is the act of blessing that is emphasised by causing the stress to fall upon the verb – 'God *bless* thee'. The child who is speaking in the poem may invoke God, but Blake's point is that it is the child's own frame of mind that makes both his and the lamb's state blessed, and he makes the metre hint at that point.

The nine-line stanzas of 'Spring' have a much more elaborate rhythmical pattern. Each of the first eight lines has only three syllables, in a stressed, unstressed, stressed, sequence. There is a standard metrical foot of three syllables with that stress pattern, called an amphimacer. The ninth line then has twelve syllables, arranged as two amphimacers (the stress on the last syllable of 'Merrily' is lighter than that on the first, but it still fits the pattern followed by three iambic feet. This is a complicated structure, and one that makes stressed syllables greatly outnumber unstressed ones: each stanza has 36 syllables, of which 23 are stressed and only 13 unstressed. The movement is formal and emphatic, almost more the rhythm of a dance than of a song. What the poem says is simple enough but Blake has decorated it with a poetic artifice as lavish in its own way as are the illustrations and designs with which he has enriched the two plates that carry the text.

The combination of those two factors may well encourage the reader who sees the poem as Blake meant it to be seen, in his illuminated book, to think that perhaps it is not so slight a piece as a conventionally printed modern text allows it to appear. After all, it contains one of the main themes of the *Songs*: the importance of the empathetic ability to identify with all other creatures. That ability alone can overcome the personal isolation which will otherwise alienate the individual from the rest of creation. Blake uses a slight, but telling, manipulation of the poem's verbal structure to register the presence of this theme. The first two stanzas, in which several different kinds of bird join together with 'Little Boy' and 'Little Girl' to celebrate the coming of spring, end with 'Merrily, Merrily, to welcome in the Year.' In the third stanza, where the child who speaks embraces and kisses a lamb, involving it and himself with the others, this becomes 'Merrily, Merrily, *we* welcome in the Year.' Because Blake keeps firmly to the metrical pattern the stress falls on the first syllable of the verb and not on the pronoun, but he manages to emphasise that pronoun all the same. The refrain line is much longer than the other lines in the stanza and is quite different in structure, so it stands out sharply from those other lines. It is used twice in one form and then, suddenly, in this altered form, the alteration emphasised by the fact that 'we' and 'welcome' – subject and verb – alliterate with each other. All this is done without altering the metre.

But 'altering the metre' is something that Blake does often in *Songs of Experience*. The eight lines of 'The Sick Rose' mostly have five syllables and two stresses each (in speaking the second line of the poem 'The' is elided or slurred into the first syllable of 'invisible', keeping the count at five). But when the brief drama enacted by the poem begins to reveal its meaning in lines six and seven they have four syllables and six respectively. This preserves the normal total of ten for the two lines taken together but it does break the pattern. Also, however you try to distribute the stresses amongst the syllables of 'And his dark secret love' it seems to have more than two, perhaps as many as four. This combines with the fact that it is irregularly long, all the more noticeably so because it comes after a line that is irregularly short, to slow down the movement of the verse, allowing these words to sink in.

'The Fly' is written in very short lines of either three or four syllables. Normally, the shorter the lines of a poem are, the more strongly the verse pattern impresses itself on the reader's inner ear. But look at how Blake has distributed those line lengths through the five stanzas of this poem:

Stanzas one,
two, and
three –   three
                  four
                  four
                  four

Stanza four –   four
                  four
                  three
                  four

Stanza five –   three
                  four
                  three
                  four

Three stanzas are probably enough for a pattern to register in the reader's mind, so Blake shifts the pattern in stanza four and then shifts it again in stanza five. Moreover, the rhyme scheme works to disguise the shortness of the lines. The eight short lines in each stanza of 'Spring' are rhymed in couplets, which very firmly impresses on the ear both their brevity and their place in a poetic pattern (such pairings as 'crow/you' and 'lick/neck' are only half-rhymes, but are still close enough to be heard). In the stanzas of 'The Fly' only lines two and four rhyme, so the ear tends not to 'hear' the lines as being as short as they actually are. Despite what the *eye* sees as a very 'tight' verse form, the poem sounds on the *ear* like speech, even like conversation.

In 'Ah! Sun-flower' Blake even makes so inherently artificial a metrical form as the anapaest sound like speech. An anapaestic foot has three syllables, the first two unstressed and the third stressed, and each line of 'Ah! Sun-flower' consists of three such feet. The first two lines of the poem,however, do not allow that metrical norm to establish itself because they only have eight syllables. The first, unstressed, syllable has been left off (line seven is the same). At least two of the other lines are metrically ambiguous. 'Virgin' would normally be pronounced with a stress on its first syllable, but where it stands in line six the metre works against that pronunciation, requiring at least that the stresses either side of it, on 'pale' and on the first syllable of 'shrouded', should be stronger. Similarly 'Seeking' has a stressed first syllable, but it stands as the first word in line three, where the metre would not allow a full stress until the first syllable of 'after'. Later in the same line 'golden' causes a similar difficulty. These difficulties can be resolved, but the reader will probably resolve them by allowing normal speech patterns to modify the metrical pattern. Again, as with 'The Fly', the verse is moved away from song and towards talk.

These formal distinctions that I am drawing between the poems in the two groups should not be pushed too far for they are not absolute. The *Innocence* 'Nurse's Song' is written in anapaests that are if anything even more freely resolved than are those of 'Ah! Sun-flower', and 'The Little Vagabond' moves more lightly than most of the *Songs of Experience* do. But these differences do emerge clearly enough over the two groups taken as a whole, and they do so to some point. Consider these passages selected from *Songs of Experience*:

> Is that trembling cry a song?
> Can it be a song of joy?
> And so many children poor?
> It is a land of poverty!
> ('Holy Thursday')

And the gates of this Chapel were shut,
And 'Thou shalt not' writ over the door . . . .
('The Garden of Love')

I wander thro' each charter'd street,
Near where the charter'd Thames does flow,
And mark in every face I meet
Marks of weakness, marks of woe.
('London')

Pity would be no more
If we did not make somebody Poor;
And Mercy no more could be
If all were as happy as we.
('The Human Abstract')

These are examples of what could be described as a kind of helpless rhetorical gesturing *at* the problems rather than a saying of anything very constructive about what might be done about them. The commentary on the poems has shown that some such positive suggestions do emerge from them, but by implication, obliquely, rather than by direct statement. The direct 'surface' statements of many of the *Songs of Experience* are matters of angry questioning, voiced in the accents of passionate speech. By contrast the *Songs of Innocence* are most often celebrating something, and it is entirely appropriate that they should do so to the sound of music. It is too easy, and too limiting, simply to conclude that what can be seen as a greater flexibility in the versification of what are, after all, later poems, shows the improvement in Blake's technical skill as a poet between 1788 and 1794 and leave it at that. The two groups of poems are doing different things, and the difference between their styles is the result of that.

5.3 IMAGERY

In the first two stanzas of 'A Little Boy Lost' structure, language, and imagery combine to create the effect that Blake wants. The reasoning behind those stanzas is intellectually complex. Look again at the passages quoted in the commentary on the poem from *Jerusalem* and *The Everlasting Gospel* (see section 4.2), and from Blake's notes on Swedenborg, to see how much so it is, and how involved Blake's articulation of it can be. But in 'A Little Boy Lost' Blake is careful to make the expression of these ideas convincingly childlike. It is true that he is more successful in the second stanza than in the first, but that fact in itself means that as the reader moves through the poem the impression of this being a child's point of view is built up in his mind. The one concrete image in the first two stanzas then works to complete that impression, for it is just such an image as a child might pick on:

> I love you like the little bird
> That picks up crumbs around the door.

The image is not mere decoration. It says something, and it also works to persuade the reader to accept what it says.

In its precision and its realism that image is typical of Blake, for he put a high value on specificity in art. In Chapter 3 of *Jerusalem* he asserts that 'every Minute Particular is Holy', and he argues that in art, in science, and even in the operation of human kindness, close attention to such minute particulars is all important:

He who would do good to another must do it in Minute
    Particulars:
General Good is the plea of the scoundrel, hypocrite &
    flatterer,
For Art & Science cannot exist but in minutely organized
    Particulars
And not in generalizing Demonstrations of the Rational Power.

'Vision ' is not achieved by departing from reality but is rather a heightened and intensified awareness of the precise details of individual reality, 'so he who wishes to see a Vision, a perfect Whole,/ Must see it in its Minute Particulars, Organized' (*Jerusalem*, Chapter 4). It is for such reasons that the detail of 'their innocent faces clean' in the first line of the *Innocence* 'Holy Thursday' warrants the importance that I attach to it in my commentary on the poem. It is not a casual remark but an observation with a purpose behind it, a purpose revealed by the minute particulars of that poem itself, and of its relationship both to its *Experience* contrary and to other poems in the cycle.

Blake's images are constantly made to work in this kind of way for their employment. The evocation of the 'New worlds' in the last two stanzas of 'Night' is openly unrealistic. Blake may have drawn his symbols from so familiar a source as Isaiah's vision of a restored Israel as the kingdom of heaven on earth partly in order to stress that this is a different world from the one he and his readers are living in. But the second stanza of the poem works differently:

> Farewell, green fields and happy groves,
> Where flocks have took delight.
> Where lambs have nibbled, silent moves
> The feet of angels bright;
> Unseen they pour blessing
> And joy without ceasing,
> On each bud and blossom,
> And each sleeping bosom.

In these lines 'natural' and 'supernatural' forms move through the poem on equal terms with each other, so that the reader is encouraged to think of them as equally 'real'. The 'New worlds' of the last two stanzas may not belong to this world, at least not yet, for they are an expression of the possibilities that exist within it, but what *does* belong to this world is an awareness of the reality of moral and spiritual presences that 'pour blessing', and 'pitying stand and weep'. The fact that such things are present realities justifies those future possibilities, and guarantees that they are possible. The poem's images create both the actuality and the possibility, distinguish between them, and hint at the necessary connection between them.

The imagery of such poems as 'The Sick Rose' is more difficult to interpret, seems, indeed, almost to defy straightforward 'interpretation'. Some plausible explanations can be made easily enough: the worm is a symbol of death; it and the rose are sexual symbols; the worm is 'invisible' for the naturalistic reason that it 'flies in the night,' under cover of darkness. That 'night' can then be related to the one in which, in 'Earth's Answer', conventional morality has 'Chain'd' the 'delight' of sexual love. The conclusions offered in the commentary on the poem soon begin to emerge. But push this line of interpretation far enough and it can begin to make the poem seem faintly ridiculous. There is a sense in which it is irreducibly a poem about a worm and a rose, about a natural phenomenon.

There are good reasons, however, why it should be so. Remember Blake's claim in his letter to Dr Trusler (see p. 18) that

> The wisest of the Ancients consider'd what is not too Explicit as the fittest for Instruction, because it rouzes the faculties to act.

Blake may want to 'educate' his readers, but not by way of setting down moral precepts for them to follow. If a moral conclusion does emerge from the reading of 'The Sick Rose' then it emerges in the reader's own mind, as a conclusion drawn from his own experience of working through the poem's imagery. It is a part of the reader's own actively created experience, not an externally presented and passively received suggestion. And it is experience that is actively created out of the imaginatively enhanced perception of natural phenomena. Read again section 3.1 of this book on the theme of quality of vision in Blake's poetry, especially the discussion there of the 1802 poem to Thomas Butts which defines the four levels of vision. How Blake extends and elaborates his perception of the 'frowning Thistle' in that poem is exactly how the reader of 'The Sick Rose' is encouraged, even forced, to extend and elaborate his perception of the worm and the rose.

I have argued in that section that such imaginative perception is for Blake the means by which 'the doors of perception' may be 'cleansed', and that he consistently tried to use his art

To open the Eternal Worlds, to open the immortal Eyes
Of Man inwards into the worlds of Thought, into Eternity
Ever expanding into the Bosom of God, the Human Imagination.

The uses of imagery that I have been discussing here are means to that end. Shelley wrote in *A Defence of Poetry* that 'Poetry strengthens' the imagination 'in the same manner as exercise strengthens a limb'. So it is with Blake's imagery: by rousing the reader's 'faculties to act' it aims to exercise and strengthen those faculties so that they may work the more effectively in the reader's daily life. And it is not only the imagery that is being directed towards that end: versification and language, the overall contrast between the two sets of songs, and the specific contrasts within contrary pairings of individual poems from each set, all of these things are also involved in the process. Readers who experience the differences between 'The Lamb' and 'The Tyger' are not being told about the differences between gentleness and ferocity, or between love and dread, they are *experiencing* those differences, in the movement, language, and imagery of the poems.

6 CRITICAL ANALYSIS OF A SPECIMEN POEM

This chapter should be read in conjunction with the commentary on 'London' in section 4.3.

LONDON

I wander thro' each charter'd street,
Near where the charter'd Thames does flow,
And mark in every face I meet
Marks of weakness, marks of woe.

In every cry of every Man,
In every Infant's cry of fear,
In every voice, in every ban,
The mind-forg'd manacles I hear.

How the Chimney-sweeper's cry
Every black'ning Church appalls;
And the hapless Soldier's sigh
Runs in blood down Palace walls.

But most thro' midnight streets I hear
How the youthful Harlot's curse
Blasts the new born Infant's tear,
And blights with plagues the Marriage hearse.

Much of the power of this poem's denunciation derives directly from its form. 'London' is basically written in iambic tetrameter, lines of eight syllables each, divided into four iambic feet, but no fewer than eight of the sixteen lines do not fit this pattern. The last line of the second stanza has four full stresses but it is arguable that three of them pile up on consecutive syllables, thus:

The *mind-forg'd man*acles I *hear*.

Perhaps more obviously, the last line of the first stanza, every line in the third stanza, and the second and third lines of the last stanza, all have only seven syllables of which the first is stressed. What Blake has done in these lines is simply to drop the unstressed first syllable of the iambic line, shortening it and making it begin with the emphatic 'beat' of a stressed syllable instead of the lighter sound of a regularly unstressed one.

The result of his doing this is precisely to give *emphasis* to the lines in question. In that last line of the first stanza the words 'Marks of weakness, marks of woe' are a logical culmination of what is said in the first three lines – 'while I walked about the city I saw . . .' and the last line then tells us *what* he saw – and Blake's manipulation of the metrical structure makes a dramatic climax out of them, too. The stressing of the 'marks', the telltale signs, of inadequacy and suffering, forces them upon the reader's attention, especially when note is taken of how they have been prepared for. 'Mark' has already been used, as a verb rather than a noun, in the preceding line, and that line ends with the word 'meet', setting up a pattern of alliteration on the 'm' sound that, together with the repetition and the metrical irregularity, emphasises the 'marks' still more.

That last line of the first stanza is, in addition, very symmetrically constructed, as two phrases of three words each. In each phrase the first two words are 'marks of . . .' followed by a noun to tell us 'of' what, and Blake has used two nouns that begin with the same sound, '*weakness*' and '*woe*'. This symmetrical balancing has as much to do with the line's impact as do the other features already commented on. Perhaps it also works to suggest something that the lines do not explicitly state. That elaborately patterned sequence of Marks of weakness, marks of woe' may imply not just an association but a direct, causative, link, that these people suffer *because* they are weak. In the second stanza the 'manacles' that control the citizens are 'mind-forg'd', purely mental, imaginary constraints. These people submit to their own oppression. The words of the first stanza do not say all of this, but Blake's patterning of them implies it, preparing us as we read through the poem for the more direct statement at the end of stanza two. That direct statement is then given its own kind of special emphasis by the irregular accumulation of stresses on the first three syllables of the key phrase 'mind-forg'd manacles'.

Blake now makes every line in the third stanza be of the shortened and emphatic form because here, too, he seems to be aiming at an effect of dramatic force. The first two stanzas consist essentially of generalisations. A clear sign of this is the way the second uses the word 'every' five times in just four lines and 24 words. The third and fourth stanzas then accumulate between them three specific examples of repression or exploitation and its consequences. Two of these examples are compressed into the third stanza, and the other is more expansively presented in the fourth. The insistent beat of the stressed syllables at the beginnings of all the lines of the third stanza gives weight and power to Blake's unveiling of the evidence for his indictment, an effect like that of a speaker striking with his fist on a table to emphasise his words:

> *How* the Chimney-sweeper's cry
> *Every* black'ning Church appalls;
> *And* the hapless Soldier's sigh
> *Runs* in blood down Palace walls.

After which the power of this, the second of the two shortened lines in the last stanza, hardly needs direct comment:

> *Blasts* the new born Infant's tear . . .

It is worthy of comment, though, that we know that Blake deliberately created the effect in that particular line. In the manuscript draft of the poem he originally made a perfectly regular iambic tetrameter:

> And blasts the new born infant's tear.

Dropping the initial 'And' gives the line much more impact, especially when we see from the draft that the powerful alliteration with 'blights with plagues' in the last line was equally deliberately arrived at. Blake tried both 'hangs' and 'smites with plagues' before fixing on 'blights'.

In the third stanza the chimney sweeper is an obvious enough focus of pity, but the soldier might seem surprising company for him in such a context. However, once Blake's imagination has helped ours to penetrate to the reality of his situation then the association will seem less surprising. By mentioning the 'Church' alongside the sweep Blake reminds us that something could be done about his plight, but is not being done. Similarly, the association of 'Palace walls' with the soldier reminds us that someone gives him both the licence and the orders to do the things that he does, and expects him to run the risk of being injured or killed in doing them. Blake presents these two cases in such a way as to bring out the full implications of 'mind-forg'd manacles' in the preceding stanza: such circumstances are not inescapable facts of life, they are created and maintained by human malice or indifference.

By beginning the last stanza with the words 'But *most* . . .' Blake emphasises that this is the poem's most crucial, most important, statement. The fact that this third of his specific cases is worked through the length of a whole stanza, whereas the sweep and the soldier are only allowed half a stanza each, further reflects its importance. That striking phrase 'the Marriage hearse', so striking because of its macabre variation of the expected 'marriage bed', tells us, vividly, that it is not only the underclasses of this society who suffer from its repressive nature. The lives of the 'respectable' classes, whose members marry and beget legitimate children, are also impoverished and deadened. I have already suggested that 'the youthful Harlot's curse' may be veneral disease; it certainly is a metaphor for the degradation of her life, and the whole of an organism is tainted by such degradation of any of its parts. The church is blackened by 'the Chimney-sweeper's cry', and rulers who maintain themselves in power by force stain that power with blood. The images in the second half of 'London' convert the moral and spiritual corruption of its first half into physical corruption, bringing the poem to rest in an atmosphere of darkness (the 'midnight streets'), disease, and death. To reflect this, and to reinforce it, Blake brings the poem's verbal structure to rest on the word 'hearse'.

Again the draft, archaeologically recording Blake's changes of mind as he worked on the poem, reveals the deliberation with which he worked. The first version of the final stanza was:

> But most the midnight harlot's curse
> From every dismal street I hear,
> Weaves around the marriage hearse
> And blasts the new born infant's tear.

Of course 'marriage hearse' is still a striking phrase, even at the end of the third line rather than the fourth, but the reader's attention is not so concentrated on it when it is followed by another line, nor does the verbal sequence so perfectly mirror the thematic movement. Whether or not such considerations were consciously in the forefront of Blake's mind, he set about reconstructing the stanza so as to move that phrase to the end of it, and the poem benefits from the change.

7 CRITICAL RECEPTION

At the beginning of this book I said that Blake lived, worked, and died in relative obscurity, and that 'relative' should be stressed, for he was far from totally unknown. There were even times in his life when he was almost famous, but it was as a painter and engraver and not as a poet that he was so. This bias in the interest in Blake persisted for some time. The great Victorian critic and art historian, John Ruskin, was an admirer of some of Blake's poetry, but it is said that when he acquired a fine coloured copy of *Jerusalem* he cut it up and distributed the separate plates as gifts amongst his artistic friends.

This situation was not helped by the fact that Blake's publication methods meant that there was an almost total absence of accessible printed texts. The first conventionally printed edition of *Songs of Innocence and of Experience* only appeared in 1839, and it was the work of a young Swedenborgian named Wilkinson, whose interest in the poems arose from their presentation of the reality of 'Spiritual phenomena' and who wanted to use them to promote a 'new Spiritualism'. Appreciation, and even very much actual knowledge, of Blake's poetry remained the preserve of a select few, until the publication in 1863 of the first full biography, Alexander Gilchrist's *The Life of William Blake, 'Pictor Ignotus', with Selections from His Poems and Other Writings*, in two volumes. The biographical part of the work made Blake a posthumous celebrity and the second volume, the *Selections*, at last made a substantial body of his work available in an easily obtainable form. The texts were not very accurate by scholarly standards and Victorian standards of propriety had required that some of them even be censored, but it was a start, and other editions soon began to appear.

Gilchrist's *Life* also began the necessary work of amending another, all too persistent, aspect of what interest there then was in Blake, the belief that he was, at least to some extent, mad. Henry

Crabb Robinson showed some of Blake's poems to Wordsworth around 1826, and recorded this as the poet's verdict on them:

> There is no doubt this poor man was mad, but there is something in the madness of this man which interests me more than the Sanity of Lord Byron & Walter Scott.

A belief in Blake's insanity did not, as Wordsworth's comment shows, have to involve the dismissal of his work as unworthy of attention, but it did tend to limit the seriousness of that attention. Gilchrist set out to present Blake as a unique and individual genius, rather than a madman, his apparent eccentricities the product of a truly imaginative mind:

> According to his own explanation, Blake saw spiritual appearances by the exercise of a special faculty – that of imagination – using the word in the then unusual, but true sense, of a faculty which busies itself with the subtler realities, not with fictions . . . He said the things imagination saw were as much realities as were gross and tangible facts.

The Victorian poet, Algernon Charles Swinburne, went further still in an influential book on Blake, that had begun as a review of Gilchrist's *Life* but had soon outgrown that role:

> One might almost pity the poor age and the poor men he came among for having such a fiery energy cast unawares into the midst of their small customs and competitions. Unluckily for them, their new prophet had not one point they could lay hold of, not one organ or channel of expression by which to make himself comprehensible to such as they were . . . He was born and baptized into the church of rebels; we can hardly imagine a time or scheme of things in which he could have lived and worked without some interval of revolt.

Thus was begun the work of replacing the image of Blake the lunatic with that of Blake the original, individual, genius, and, perhaps more significant in the long run, that of Blake the visionary rebel. Modern criticism has added other, related images to those two: the moral teacher, and the subtle psychologist. In short, the profound and original thinker. Blake's first really scholarly modern critic was perhaps S. Foster Damon, who published *William Blake: His Philosophy and Symbols* in 1924. The consummation of Damon's work on

Blake was his *A Blake Dictionary: The Ideas and Symbols of William Blake*, first published in 1965. In the Introduction to the *Dictionary* Damon wrote that:

> Blake's basic purpose was the discovery and recording of new truths about the human soul. For him the most exciting thing possible was the discovery of these truths. Hunting for them and warfare over them with other thinkers were the joys of his 'eternity' . . . With a few trifling exceptions, Blake never wrote a poem or painted a picture without intellectual meaning.

The early scholars and critics of Blake were primarily concerned to reclaim him as a poet whose work could appeal to the ordinary reader of poetry. That accomplished, much of the best modern criticism has concerned itself with the ways in which, as Damon puts it, 'Blake is a challenge to every thinking person.' This 'professionalisation' of Blake studies has achieved the full assimilation of Blake into the mainstream of English literary history, even of English cultural life, and has produced an increasingly learned and subtle scholarship devoted to the elucidation of Blake's thought. Amongst the works listed in the Further Reading, Damon's *A Blake Dictionary* and Erdman's *The Illuminated Blake* are outstanding products of that professioinal scholarship – indispensable tools for the student of Blake's work.

Although most readers of Blake probably come to know him through the *Songs*, much of this criticism has, understandably enough, tended to concentrate on the longer and more complex poems. In his *Blake's Apocalypse* (1963) Harold Bloom actually complains that the *Songs* 'continue to usurp something of the study which should be given to Blake's more ambitious and greater works'. By treating the shorter poems as component parts of a large, unified, symbolic and prophetic system, critics such as Bloom and Hazard Adams have successfully shown the consistencies in the patterns of thought that lie behind all of Blake's work. It is an approach which, incautiously applied, can lead to reading the lyrics in too rigid and schematic a fashion, and some critics have objected to it on those grounds. Used with caution, however, this approach has revealed deeper and wider significances in the *Songs* than were apparent to their nineteenth-century admirers. In writing this Guide I have indicated what I take to be the important points of relationship between the *Songs* and the other works in which Blake further developed and refined his 'Visionary forms dramatic' (*Jerusalem*, Chapter 4).

REVISION QUESTIONS

1. Using a facsimile of the *Songs*, preferably in colour, consider what significances, if any, you can find in the relationship between texts and designs in the cases of: 'Infant Joy'; 'Spring'; 'The Little Vagabond'; 'The Sick Rose'; and, both separately and as a pair, 'The Lamb, and 'The Tyger'.

2. 'The wisest of the Ancients consider'd what is not too Explicit as the fittest for Instruction, because it rouzes the faculties to act' (Blake, letter to Dr Trusler). Consider how Blake's own works rouse their readers' 'faculties to act.'

3. Would you agree with D. W. Harding that Blake's poetry is 'exploring the relation between the perfect possibilities he felt in human life and the lamentable confusions and imperfections that appear in actual experience'?

4. 'Man's perceptions are not bounded by organs of perception; he percieves more than sense (tho' ever so acute) can discover' (Blake, *There is No Natural Religion*). Discuss the *Songs* in the light of this claim.

5. In *The Marriage of Heaven and Hell* Blake writes of 'the desire of raising other men into a perception of the infinite'. Do you think that the *Songs* are motivated by this desire?

6. Would you agree that Blake's central theme was the need to release the human spirit from bondage?

7. In *A Vision of the Last Judgment* Blake wrote that 'Those who are cast out' from heaven 'are All Those who, having no Passions

of their own . . . Have spent their lives in Curbing & Governing other People's by the Various arts of Poverty & Cruelty of all kinds.' Does this comment offer a useful perspective on the *Songs*?

8. 'The *Songs of Innocence and of Experience* . . . are the poems of a man with a profound interest in human emotions, and a profound knowledge of them' (T. S. Eliot). Which of the *Songs* could be used as evidence to support that claim, and why?

9. Blake insisted that in his poetry 'Every word and every letter is studied and put into its fit place; the terrific numbers are reserved for the terrific parts, the mild & gentle for the mild & gentle parts'. Consider the appropriateness of style to subject matter in: 'The Chimney Sweeper' (both versions); 'A Cradle Song'; 'Holy Thursday' (both versions); 'The Fly'; 'The Tyger'; 'A Poison Tree'; and 'The Voice of the Ancient Bard'.

10. Consider how the *Songs* present the inadequacies of existing society and of the quality of life which it promotes.

11. Look at the pairs of contrary poems and consider what difference it makes in each case to how you read any one poem when you read it alongside its contrary rather than by itself.

FURTHER READING

Texts and sources

Every student of Blake should try to examine a good facsimile of his illuminated text. A colour facsimile of *Songs of Innocence and of Experience*, with introduction and commentary by Geoffrey Keynes, was published as an Oxford University Press paperback in 1970. Oxford University Press also published David V. Erdman's *The Illuminated Blake*, which reproduces the entire illustrated canon in one volume, in 1975. The facsimiles are only in black and white but Erdman's commentary on the designs is extensive and detailed.

Reference has frequently been made in this Guide to the notebook (sometimes known as the 'Rossetti Manuscript', since it was owned for a while by the Victorian poet and painter Dante Gabriel Rossetti) used by Blake between about 1793 and 1811. It contains drafts, some of them much altered in the writing, of many of the *Songs of Experience*, together with other poems written at about the same time and on similar themes. You will find this material helpful and interesting in your study of the *Songs*, and you should consult one of the comprehensive editions of Blake's work that include transcriptions of these texts, such as the Oxford University Press *Complete Writings*, edited by Geoffrey Keynes and first published in 1966, or the Penguin *Complete Poems*, edited by Alicia Ostriker and first published in 1977. Keynes also edited a facsimile of the notebook itself for the Nonesuch Press in 1935.

Biographies

Gilchrist's *Life of William Blake* is still worth reading, but it is not entirely accurate. The edition prepared by Ruthven Todd for Dent's Everyman Library in 1942 has notes which make the necessary corrections. Mona Wilson's *The Life of William Blake*, first published in 1927 by the Nonesuch Press, is more up to date, especially since it has been revised for later editions. The most recent of these revisions was prepared by Geoffrey Keynes for the Oxford University Press in 1971, and is available as a paperback.

Critical works

Thereis an enormous amount and variety of Blake criticism available, and much of it is good. Blake has, on the whole, been very fortunate in his critics. The following is a brief, and very selective, list of specific recommendations:

Adams, Hazard, *William Blake, a Reading of the Shorter Poems* (University of Washington Press, 1963).

Blackstone, Bernard, *English Blake* (Cambridge University Press, 1949).

Bloom, Harold, *Blake's Apocalypse: A Study in Poetic Argument* (Gollancz, 1963).

Bronowski, J., *William Blake and the Age of Revolution* (Routledge & Kegan Paul, 1972). Relates the poems to their political and social context.

Damon, S. Foster, *A Blake Dictionary: The Ideas and Symbols of William Blake* (Thames & Hudson, 1973). Indispensable for the serious student of Blake.

Erdman, David V., *Blake, Prophet Against Empire* (Princeton University Press, 1954). Like Bronowski's book, this one sets the poems into a historical context, but it does so in more thoroughgoing detail.

Frye, Northrop, *Fearful Symmetry* (Princeton University Press, 1947).

Gillham, D. G., *Blake's Contrary States: The 'Songs of Innocence and of Experience' as Dramatic Poems* (Cambridge University Press, 1966).

Raine, Kathleen, *William Blake* (Thames & Hudson, 1970). A concise and accessible study of Blake's work as a visual artist, which relates that work to the writings, and to the relevant events of Blake's life.

Mastering English Literature
Richard Gill

Mastering English Literature will help readers both to enjoy English Literature and to be successful in 'O' levels, 'A' levels and other public exams. It is an introduction to the study of poetry, novels and drama which helps the reader in four ways - by providing ways of approaching literature, by giving examples and practice exercises; by offering hints on how to write about literature, and by the author's own evident enthusiasm for the subject. With extracts from more than 200 texts, this is an enjoyable account of how to get the maximum satisfaction out of reading, whether it be for formal examinations or simply for pleasure.

Work Out English Literature ('A' level)
S.H. Burton

This book familiarises 'A' level English Literature candidates with every kind of test which they are likely to encounter. Suggested answers are worked out step by step and accompanied by full author's commentary. The book helps students to clarify their aims and establish techniques and standards so that they can make appropriate responses to similar questions when the examination pressures are on. It opens up fresh ways of looking at the full range of set texts, authors and critical judgements and motivates students to know more of these matters.

THE MACMILLAN SHAKESPEARE

General Editor: PETER HOLLINDALE
Advisory Editor: PHILIP BROCKBANK

The Macmillan Shakespeare features:
* clear and uncluttered texts with modernised punctuation and spelling wherever possible;
* full explanatory notes printed on the page facing the relevant text for ease of reference;
* stimulating introductions which concentrate on content, dramatic effect, character and imagery, rather than mere dates and sources.

Above all, The Macmillan Shakespeare treats each play as a work for the theatre which can also be enjoyed on the page.

CORIOLANUS
Editor: Tony Parr

THE WINTER'S TALE
Editor: Christopher Parry

MUCH ADO ABOUT NOTHING
Editor: Jan McKeith

RICHARD II
Editor: Richard Adams

RICHARD III
Editor: Richard Adams

HENRY IV, PART I
Editor: Peter Hollindale

HENRY IV, PART II
Editor: Tony Parr

HENRY V
Editor: Brian Phythian

AS YOU LIKE IT
Editor: Peter Hollindale

A MIDSUMMER NIGHT'S DREAM
Editor: Norman Sanders

THE MERCHANT OF VENICE
Editor: Christopher Parry

THE TAMING OF THE SHREW
Editor: Robin Hood

TWELFTH NIGHT
Editor: E. A. J. Honigmann

THE TEMPEST
Editor: A. C. Spearing

ROMEO AND JULIET
Editor: James Gibson

JULIUS CAESAR
Editor: D. R. Elloway

MACBETH
Editor: D. R. Elloway

HAMLET
Editor: Nigel Alexander

ANTONY AND CLEOPATRA
Editors: Jan McKeith and
Richard Adams

OTHELLO
Editors: Celia Hilton and R. T. Jones

KING LEAR
Editor: Philip Edwards